Growing Mathematical Minds

Growing Mathematical Minds translates the findings of developmental psychological research related to early mathematics into narratives that are meaningful to teachers and readily applicable in early childhood classrooms. This highly useful book bridges the gap between research and practice, supporting teachers to adopt evidence-based practices and improve teaching by applying cutting-edge research findings. *Growing Mathematical Minds* describes findings that will affect teaching in ways that help children from three to eight years develop foundational math knowledge and skills, positive attitudes toward math, and basic abilities to think mathematically.

Jennifer S. McCray is a research scientist and the Principal Investigator of the Early Math Collaborative at Erikson Institute.

Jie-Qi Chen is the Founder of the Early Math Collaborative, and Senior Vice President for Academic Affairs and Dean of Faculty at Erikson Institute.

Janet Eisenband Sorkin is a research scientist in early childhood math education at the University of Chicago.

Other Eye On Education Books
Available from Routledge
(www.routledge.com/eyeoneducation)

Coding as a Playground:
Programming and Computational Thinking in the
Early Childhood Classroom
Marina Umaschi Bers

Eco-Education for Young Children:
Revolutionary Ways to Teach and Learn Environmental Sciences
Ann Lewin-Benham

The Bridge to School:
Aligning Teaching with Development for Ages Four to Six
Claire Bainer, Liisa Hale, and Gail Myers

Teaching Children with Challenging Behaviors:
Practical Strategies for Early Childhood Educators
Edited by Gayle Mindes

Anti-Bias Education in the Early Childhood Classroom:
Hand in Hand, Step by Step
Katie Kissinger

Developing Natural Curiosity through Project-Based Learning:
Five Strategies for the PreK-3 Classroom
Dayna Laur and Jill Ackers

Five Teaching and Learning Myths-Debunked:
A Guide for Teachers
Adam Brown and Althea Need Kaminske

Nurturing Young Thinkers Across the Standards:
K-2
Wynne A. Shilling and Sydney L. Schwartz

Growing Mathematical Minds

Conversations Between Developmental Psychologists and Early Childhood Teachers

Edited by Jennifer S. McCray, Jie-Qi Chen,
and Janet Eisenband Sorkin

Routledge
Taylor & Francis Group

NEW YORK AND LONDON

First published 2019
by Routledge
711 Third Avenue, New York, NY 10017

and by Routledge
2 Park Square, Milton Park, Abingdon, Oxon, OX14 4RN

Routledge is an imprint of the Taylor & Francis Group, an informa business

© 2019 Taylor & Francis

The right of Jennifer S. McCray, Jie-Qi Chen, and Janet Eisenband
Sorkin to be identified as the authors of the editorial material, and of
the authors for their individual chapters, has been asserted in
accordance with sections 77 and 78 of the Copyright, Designs and
Patents Act 1988.

All rights reserved. No part of this book may be reprinted or
reproduced or utilised in any form or by any electronic, mechanical,
or other means, now known or hereafter invented, including
photocopying and recording, or in any information storage or
retrieval system, without permission in writing from the publishers.

Trademark notice: Product or corporate names may be trademarks or
registered trademarks, and are used only for identification and
explanation without intent to infringe. Printed in Canada.

Library of Congress Cataloging-in-Publication Data
Names: McCray, Jennifer S., editor. | Chen, Jie-Qi, editor. |
    Eisenband-Sorkin, Janet, editor.
Title: Growing mathematical minds : conversations between
    developmental psychologists and early childhood teachers / edited
    by Jennifer S. McCray, Jie-Qi Chen, and Janet Eisenband-Sorkin.
Description: New York, NY : Routledge, 2018. | Includes
    bibliographical references and index.
Identifiers: LCCN 2018007108 (print) | LCCN 2018019662 (ebook) |
    ISBN 9781315646497 (e-book) | ISBN 9781138182363 (hardback) |
    ISBN 9781138182370 (pbk.)
Subjects: LCSH: Mathematics—Study and teaching (Elementary) |
    Mathematics teachers—Training of. | Elementary school teachers—
    Training of. | Developmental psychobiology.

ISBN: 978-1-138-18236-3 (hbk)
ISBN: 978-1-138-18237-0 (pbk)
ISBN: 978-1-315-64649-7 (ebk)

Typeset in Palatino
by Apex CoVantage, LLC

Contents

Acknowledgements

As authors, and as educators, we have had the great good fortune to work at Erikson Institute and within the confines of the Early Math Collaborative. There are many staff and students who have contributed indirectly to the work we have been able to produce here, and we are very grateful to them all.

We have also worked directly with many early childhood teachers over the past 10 years. They are our heroes, and inspire our work every day. For this volume, we are especially grateful to sixteen wonderful teachers who were generous with both their time and their thoughts in ways that made this work possible. They include: Emily Anderson, Nancy Ansorge, Jane Averill, Amanda Burns, Toni Galassini, Rosalba Granados, Megan Hillegass, Glenna Jakush, Priscella Lindsey, Cindi Lopardo, Lisa Matuska, Jessica Petertil, Lauren Putze, Juana Resendiz, Jill Sapoznick, and Liz Watras.

We'd like to thank them here for their invaluable contribution to this book, and hope they will feel well-represented and proud of what we accomplished together.

–The author/editor team

Introduction: Bridging the Gap Between Research and Practice in Early Mathematics

Jie-Qi Chen, Jennifer S. McCray, and Janet Eisenband Sorkin

This book reflects an innovative, collaborative effort to translate the findings of developmental psychological research related to early mathematics into terms that are meaningful to teachers and readily applicable in early childhood classrooms. The book is an attempt to **bridge the gap** between research and practice, making it possible for teachers to adopt evidence-based practices and improve teaching, and for researchers to use teachers' applied knowledge and expertise to inform their further work. The term **early mathematics** in this book refers to experiences designed to help children from three to eight years develop foundational math knowledge and skills, positive attitudes toward math, and basic abilities to think mathematically.

Contributors to this edited volume represent three distinct groups of professionals who work to advance the field of early mathematics: **teacher educators** who devote their time and expertise to preparing teachers to provide high quality early mathematical education; **developmental psychologists** who engage in scientific studies of the conceptual and behavioral changes young children experience as they learn mathematics; and **classroom teachers** who work with such children daily to improve their mathematical knowledge and understanding. To create the book, these three groups of contributors—diverse in background and perspective—engaged in conversations focused on a common theme: developing and implementing research-based classroom practice to nurture mathematical minds in the critical early years. This book is the result of those conversations.

Teacher Educators: The Motivation to Produce the Book

The primary authors of this book are a group of early math teacher educators who have been working together—along with the book's editorial team—for a decade at Erikson Institute's Early Math Collaborative (the Collaborative; http://earlymath.erikson.edu). Launched in 2007, the Collaborative aims to transform the understanding, teaching, and learning of early mathematics from the ground up. As a team, we have spent the last 10 years working intensively alongside classroom teachers to implement and improve early math education. Through this work, we have made two specific realizations that gave rise to the idea for this book.

The first realization was the need for **translation** of early math research. As teacher educators, we strive to help teachers improve classroom practice based on relevant research in early mathematics. Through our work, we have realized how often research and practice related to early math learning do not intersect, and that teachers know little about the available research and its implications. While developmental psychologists are generally very interested in contributing to classroom practice, the influence of their early math research on practice is limited by three major factors:

- ◆ The most significant research articles are usually published in specialized journals in the fields of child development and developmental psychology. Few early childhood teachers have ready access to these journals.

- ◆ Educational implications described at the end of these research articles are often written in terms of general principles, which are thought-provoking but not always easy to connect to the specifics of daily classroom learning experiences and routines. Application in the context of ongoing classroom activity is vital for affecting change in teacher practices.

- ◆ Researchers and teachers use distinct vocabularies and expressions. Work written by scholars for an academic audience requires translation into terms that are relevant and meaningful in the field of practice. Understanding how research relates to their practice necessarily precedes teachers' implementation.

The second realization we made is the striking absence of **teacher voices** in the world of early math research. The research-to-practice process is largely unidirectional. That is, developmental psychologists are the research initiators, knowledge generators, and information disseminators. Yet, as highly sophisticated and skillful professionals, teachers are often true experts in child development in the classroom context. They have important founts of knowledge that are seldom tapped by researchers, leaving the research less well-connected to the realities of teaching and learning environments. Supporting the formation of bidirectional relationships that include dialogue and partnerships between developmental psychologists and classroom teachers is of critical importance for promoting the application of research to practice. The field of early mathematics education is more effectively advanced with the active involvement of classroom teachers.

Acting on these two realizations, the Early Math Collaborative team committed to producing a book that would address the need for greater bi-directional communication. We planned to do this by helping teachers become aware enough of the research that they could both apply it and react to it. We hoped their reactions would inform and guide the thinking of researchers, making their future research more relevant to the context of the classroom and the needs of teachers and children.

In this book we present a rich body of research, selected specifically for its potential to improve early math teaching practice. Topics and representative researchers for each chapter were selected by the Collaborative author/editor team. Over the years, members of the Collaborative have developed a shared understanding of foundational mathematics, early childhood teaching, and adult learning that helped us conceptualize and write this book as a group project. To ensure consistency and coherence, the same general structure was applied to all chapters. Specifically, each consists of three major sections: *(1) what the research says, (2) teachers respond to the research, and (3) teachers' ideas for classroom practice.*

Developmental Psychologists: Early Math Research Presented in the Book

Seven developmental psychologists participated in this book project. They were invited because the research they conduct relates to a critical issue in early math education, has clear implications for classroom practice, and focuses on big ideas in pedagogy; as a group, their work represents a wide range of early math teaching and learning topics. In some cases, the researcher was involved in every study that was cited; in others, researchers directed chapter authors to the work of colleagues whose findings were important to the topic. Regardless, the rigorous early math studies reported on here are original and thought-provoking.

Below we describe briefly the seven research topics in the order of the chapters presented in the book. The chapters are loosely organized based on the predominant ages of the children with whom the developmental psychologists worked. In the first few chapters, for example, the research largely focuses on the mathematical thinking and behavior of preschoolers. Research studies in the last several chapters include more early elementary students.

- ◆ *Mathematical language and early math learning with Susan Levine.* Over the past forty years, there has been remarkable work demonstrating the influence of the language to which infants and young children are exposed on their cognitive development. In this chapter, we focus on demonstrated relationships between math-related language and children's math learning.

- ◆ *The role of adult and environmental input in children's math learning with Kelly Mix.* Learning does not occur through language alone, but often involves objects, situations, and environments that facilitate the development of key ideas for young children. This chapter explores evidence that structural and visual/spatial features can help children make mathematical connections.

- ◆ *The use of concrete objects in early math learning with David Uttal.* Manipulatives have long been a common feature of early childhood classrooms. From Froebel's "gifts" and Montessori's tools, to building blocks and props for dramatic play, it is an assumption that such "handle-able" objects designed for children's use help to develop their thinking. In this chapter, we examine what is known about how manipulatives relate to children's mathematical learning in particular.

◆ *The role of gesture in teaching and learning math with Susan Goldin-Meadow.* Educators are generally aware of how what they say (and do not say) affects children's learning, but most have not thought carefully about the use of gesture—an alternate, and pervasive mode of communication—in teaching and learning. In this chapter, we study remarkable evidence about what gesture use indicates about understanding, and what its effects can be in teaching mathematics.

◆ *Variability in children's mathematical thinking and learning with Robert Siegler.* Mathematical thinking is truly developmental, with new, more sophisticated strategies for solving problems built upon labor-intensive, but "simpler" methods. This chapter brings a microgenetic lens to the study of children's strategy use and math learning in childhood, demonstrating how complicated and variable the course of strategy development is for any given child, and suggesting the importance of having multiple strategies from which to select at any time.

◆ *Pathways to number operations fluency with Arthur Baroody.* This chapter takes a deep dive into what we now know about how children develop fluency in number operations. These findings clarify the importance of a meaning-focused approach in which children's own thinking and experience work as a driver of fluency development.

◆ *Math anxiety and math performance with Erin Maloney.* Research is clear that math anxiety exists among many people, and that in some instances, it appears to "migrate" harmfully from adults to the children they interact with. This chapter explores what we know about how math anxiety functions, and suggests ways to lessen its effects.

The relevance of these research findings to early mathematics teaching and learning is obvious. Presenting them together provides the reader with an overview of developmental research with implications for early mathematics. As well, it allows the reader to compare and contrast different studies to better understand the opportunities and issues that accompany translating research into practice. Each of the chapters delves into the origins of each developmental psychologist's ideas for this particular line of research—how they became interested in the topic, what motivated them to study it, and how they pursued it through a carefully designed series of studies. Many researchers related their initial interest to a seminar or mentor in their graduate program and their own personal experience with math learning. These stories contextualize the origins of research, revealing its personal meaning and historical roots.

Classroom Teachers: The Meaning of Research for Classroom Practice

In this book, we include the voices and perspectives of 16 early childhood teachers who serve children from pre-kindergarten through third grade in different Chicago schools. All 16 teachers had previously participated in professional development sessions designed and facilitated by the Early Math Collaborative team at Erikson. While varying in terms of their teaching experience, the student population they work with, and the educational settings they work in, all the teachers share a common characteristic—a strong interest in and passion for helping young children learn foundational mathematics.

As part of the book writing process, the teachers participated in an early mathematics research seminar at Erikson, consisting of seven two-hour sessions. In the seminar, teachers worked with the book's author team to (1) **learn about what the research says**, specifically the research of the seven selected developmental psychologists who study mathematical thinking in young children; (2) **engage in conversations** with the developmental psychologists by posing questions to them for clarification and elaboration relevant to classroom teaching; and (3) **suggest ideas for classroom practice** based on the research findings reported in the chapter. Before each seminar session, teachers read a summary of the relevant research, augmented by the input and perspective of the developmental psychologist involved. In response, teachers wrote about their understanding of the research, their questions for the researcher, and their thoughts about translating the research findings into classroom teaching.

Teacher activities during each seminar session were based on the research topic presented in the chapter. For example, during the session that focused on the work of Erin Maloney on math anxiety, each teacher created an autobiography sharing their personal experience of math learning and the feelings associated with it. During the seminar session about David Uttal's work on the use of concrete objects in early math teaching and learning, teachers explored a variety of math manipulatives to examine their different functions. As appropriate, teachers watched video clips during seminar sessions to enhance their understanding of the concepts discussed in a particular chapter. Other times, teachers worked together to solve a series of math problems that the developmental psychologists had used in their research studies. In all seminar sessions, teachers actively described their understanding of the research, reported the questions it prompted, and provided their thoughts about how the results could be used to support instructional practice. All seminar sessions were audiotaped and transcribed. Excerpts of teachers' comments were culled from both their written responses and the seminar transcripts, and were integrated into all three major sections of each chapter.

Teacher responses included throughout the book serve one of four purposes: 1) connecting the research to the lived experience of teaching; 2) pointing out to researchers where further explication is needed to connect the work to teaching practice; 3) asking researchers about related and classroom-pertinent topics; and 4) offering ideas and suggestions for how the work can be incorporated into early childhood classrooms. For example, in Chapter 1, on math-related language, a teacher commented that the findings presented were "backing up with research what I think most teachers have been seeing for years." Having read deeply about work on how teacher language use impacts child learning, they asked "What is the role of math-related language that children produce? Do we know whether it is equally important that children use these words themselves?" And one teacher response described the usefulness of thinking ahead about the math-related language that might naturally come up around any activity (such as "less and more" at the sand table) in order to be better prepared to provide it when it is most natural and connected to what a child is engaged in. Such comments and questions situate the work within classroom life powerfully and usefully, reflecting teachers' knowledge of how young children behave and what it takes to move beyond classroom management to intentional teaching.

The Bottom Line

In this edited book, developmental research studies of early math are described, interpreted, and applied through conversations and recommendations that target classroom teaching, teacher education, and curriculum development. The deliberate choice of this integrated approach is intended to advance early mathematics education by translating rigorous research findings into terms meaningful to teachers, with clear implications for instructional practice. At the same time, this dialogue helps researchers see how their work connects to the context of classrooms, prompting them to think about the implications of their work in a more specific and informed way. It is our intention that the book will help meet the need so clearly stated by the National Research Council to draw the attention of "individuals throughout the early childhood education system—including the teaching workforce, curriculum developers, program directors, and policy makers—to transform their approaches to mathematics education in early childhood by supporting, developing, and implementing research-based practice and curricula" (NRC, 2009, p. 3).

Going forward, we hope that this book serves as an invitation for engaging in dialogue and building partnerships in early mathematics between developmental psychologists and classroom teachers. This partnership is not about bringing research to practice alone, but is also about supporting a dynamic relationship between the two (Tseng, Easton, & Supplee, 2017). In this interaction, teachers' voices and practice concerns can help drive research at the outset and throughout its process. Together, developmental psychologists and teachers can create both new teaching ideas and more informed research questions. Based on responses from all the contributors to this volume, such partnership experiences can be transformational, leading to rich outcomes for both research and teaching. This book is only a very small step toward this goal, but we hope it suggests the power of such interactions for improving both the knowledge and the practice that serve the mathematical learning of young children.

References

National Research Council. (2009). *Mathematics learning in early childhood: Paths toward excellence and equity.* Washington, DC: National Academy Press.

Tseng, V., Easton, J. Q., and Supplee, L. H. (2017). Research-practice partnerships: Building two-way streets of engagement. *SRCD, Social Policy Report, 30*(4).

1

Mathematical Language and Early Math Learning

Janet Eisenband Sorkin and Jennifer S. McCray, with Susan Levine

Early childhood classrooms are increasingly placing emphasis on language arts and mathematics. Often these are seen as separate topics, taught in different lessons with different goals. New research indicates, however, that they may be more closely connected than many people think, particularly for young children.

For this chapter, we interviewed Susan Levine, a professor of psychology at the University of Chicago. Levine studies the development of mathematics skills in young children from a wide range of socio-economic backgrounds. One area of her research—the one we focus on here—is the role that language plays in the development of mathematical skills.

What the Research Says

The Role of Language in Math Problems

Levine told us that her interest in the relationship between language and mathematics originated from a study she conducted about calculation abilities in children from different socio-economic backgrounds.

In this study, Levine and colleagues gave kindergartners three different kinds of addition and subtraction problems involving small numbers (up to six), two verbal and one non-verbal. The first type of verbal problem used a question given verbally in the form of a "word problem." For example, the problem 3-1 was posed using a question such as *"Kim had 3 crayons. She lost 1. How many crayons did she have left?"* The second type of verbal problem was in the form of a "number fact" problem—for example, *"How much is 3 take away 1?"* These problems were classified as "verbal" because they used mathematical vocabulary, including number words (e.g., "three" and "one"), and words or phrases describing addition or subtraction (e.g., "how much," "have left," and "take away"). Further, children gave their answers verbally.

The third type of problem was considered "non-verbal": these problems did not require understanding of mathematical language. Instead of using a verbal question, the problems were presented using physical materials, including a collection of disks, a cover, and two mats. The adult and child sat facing each other, each with a mat in front of them. The adult used her mat to show the child the problem, and then the child showed the "answer" on her own mat (see Figure 1.1). For example, to ask the child to solve problem "3-1," the adult completed the following steps:

1. Placed three disks on her mat in full view of the child
2. Covered the three disks with a small box
3. Removed one disk from under the cover (as child watched)
4. Asked the child to use disks to make his mat the same as hers (which remained covered)

To succeed on this task, the child needed to observe carefully and mentally calculate how many disks should be left under the adult's cover. Notice that the child did *not*, at least on the face of it, need to be able to comprehend or use mathematical language in order to succeed.

The researchers' first finding was that children from low-income families attained lower scores than those from middle-income families on the *verbal* math tasks. This finding was not surprising, since many other studies show that lower socio-economic status (SES) is related to poorer language skills and academic achievement. The finding that *was* surprising was that on the *non-verbal* math tasks, low-income

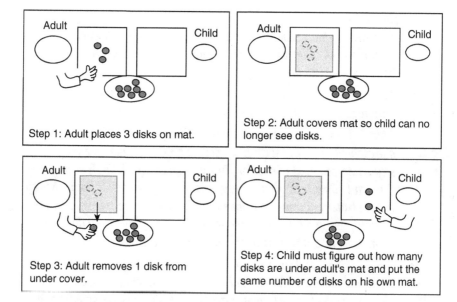

Figure 1.1 Illustration of the problem "3-1" presented non-verbally

children performed *just as well* as those from middle-income families: when mathematical language was not required in order to succeed, the achievement gap disappeared. Levine explains that the low-income students were able to add and subtract just like their more economically advantaged peers on problems involving small set sizes "as long as the language of mathematics did not have to be processed."

Why would low-income children perform worse than their peers when mathematical language *was* required? Levine says succeeding on the verbal problems requires "mapping the language of mathematics onto the numerical transformations." For example, a child needs to map the phrase "take away" to the process of removing one or more objects from a set. In order to do well on these problems, then, children need to have experience with mathematical language. Other studies show that low-income children tend to have less exposure to language (they often hear less language from their families, and the language they hear may include a narrower range of vocabulary and syntactic constructions), and therefore weaker language skills, than children from higher income families. Levine's research suggests that this difference in language exposure has an impact on children's language skills and hence their math performance.

Teacher Responses

◆ *This finding makes so much sense to me: In a way it's backing up with research what I think most teachers of lower-income children have been seeing for years.*

◆ *This is how I think we lose a lot of kids: because we don't give language to what they're doing.*

◆ *This definitely resonates with my teaching experience. I teach in a preschool, working with low-income families. Each year, my students need a lot of support in their language skills. It seems as if this isn't something that is emphasized and fostered at home. Many of the students in my class love to build and create things, and are actually using a lot of math concepts in their play. They don't all know how to put this into language, however.*

◆ *I find exciting and inspiring the notion that I can get a more accurate sense of what my students truly know and understand about math if I make an effort to include non-verbal tasks in my assessments and lessons. However, I also recognize what a challenge this presents, as most of how we "do" math in school relies heavily on language.*

"Math Talk" in Preschool Classrooms and Students' Math Gains

In another study, Levine and colleagues visited preschool classrooms from a diverse sample of urban schools. During the visits they audio-taped teachers interacting with their students for one hour, always including whole-group ("circle") time. The researchers then coded the tapes and kept track of the times that teachers engaged in "math talk" during that hour. Some examples of "math talk" they looked for were counting, referring to quantities of things (e.g., "Here are two blocks"), talking about a set having more or fewer objects than another set, and talking informally about adding or taking away objects from a set. The researchers also measured children's math skills at the beginning and end of that school year, including abilities with counting and shapes.

Levine and her colleagues found that there was great variety in the amount of math talk that different teachers provided during that hour. At the low end, a teacher engaged in math talk only once; at the high end, a teacher engaged in math talk 104 times. The average was 28 instances. Importantly, they found that the amount of math talk a teacher used was linked to children's growth in mathematics skills over the year. Regardless of their students' beginning skills, and regardless of which school they taught at, the teachers who talked more about math had students who gained more in math over the school year. The researchers interpreted their findings as showing that teachers' talk about mathematics increases children's math vocabulary, and having that math vocabulary in turn helps children grapple with the math concepts.

Concept Box 1.1   Cardinal Meaning of Number Words

The cardinal meaning of a number word is the quantity it describes—the "three-ness" of three. The tricky thing for children is that numbers are very handy for a lot of other uses, so sometimes we use numbers in ways that have little to do with their quantity. For example, we use number words:

◆ To practice learning the count list, with no reference to set size (e.g., "1, 2, 3, 4, 5, 6, 7, 8, 9, 10"!)

◆ As labels (e.g., the "Number 6" bus or Room 104).

◆ To mark time (e.g., "1, 2, 3, Go!" or "5, 4, 3, 2, 1, Blast off!")

◆ As reference points within established systems of measurement or ordering (e.g., "4 years old," "70 degrees," "5 o'clock.")

◆ To describe position within a sequence (1st, 2nd, 3rd . . .)

These ways of using numbers are all meaningful and important, but when young children are just learning the amount-related meaning of each number, it's most important they learn how the words designate a quantity; that is, express cardinality.

For example, when we hear the number word "three," we know that it refers to a set with three objects in it (★★★.) Likewise, we know that "three" cannot be used to describe a set with another quantity of objects, such as ★★ or ★★★★. This cardinal meaning of number words is critical to being able to understand more complex mathematical ideas, such as addition and subtraction.

Parents' Math Talk and Children's Understanding of Number Words

Levine and colleagues' next question was how *parents'* use of math language was related to children's math skills. After all, parents are the primary source of language a child hears, especially at the youngest ages.

To investigate, the researchers tracked children from toddlerhood through preschool, taking samples of the language they heard at home and then assessing math skills when they were older. Researchers visited the children and parents in their homes five times between the ages of 14 months and 30 months. Each time, they videotaped the parents and children for 90 minutes, telling the parents to interact with their child as they normally would. They then reviewed the videotapes and kept track of the number of times over the five sessions that the parent said a *number word* (e.g., "five" or "two").

As was the case in the study on preschool teachers' math talk, the researchers found a considerable variation in the amount of math talk that parents produced. Over the course of the five 90-minute sessions, some parents produced as little as 4 number words in total, while others produced as many as 257. The average was about 90 number words. The researchers found that the quantity of parent number words, as may be expected, was related to how much parents talked to a child *in general*. They also found a link between number word use and SES: the higher the family's SES, the more number words parents tended to use.

To see if parents' number word use was related to children's understanding of the cardinal meanings of number (see Concept Box 1.1), the researchers gave children a task called "Point to X" when they were 46 months old. On each test item, children were shown two sets of squares, each set containing between one and six squares (see Figure 1.2). For each pair, the child was asked to point to one of the quantities shown. For example, a child might be shown a set of three squares alongside a set of four squares, and asked to

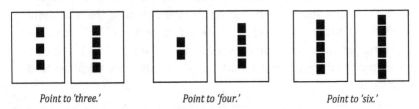

Point to 'three.'   Point to 'four.'   Point to 'six.'

Figure 1.2 Examples of "point to X" problems

"point to 'three.'" In order to succeed, the child needs to know the *cardinal* meaning of the number word "three," or *how many* the word "three" refers to. Using a series of problems, the researchers could measure the child's understanding of the cardinal meanings of number words.

The researchers found that on average, *the more number words* that were spoken by parents to their children during the videotaped sessions, *the better their children performed* on the "Point to X" task. Further, they found that this relationship held even when taking SES into account. This suggests that, just like teachers' language in classrooms, parents' talk about numbers in the home environment helps children learn about the meanings of number words. Mathematical language that children hear either at home or at school seems to help them build math skills.

Concept Box 1.2   Developing the Cardinal Principle

Understanding the *cardinal* meaning of number words (see Concept Box 2.1) is a challenging task for young children. While many children can count to 10 or even higher starting in toddlerhood, to them this task is often rote, much like reciting a poem. Even children who can point to each object in a set and give each one a number word may not know what the number words they are saying really mean. A good way to test this is to give a child a pile of objects and ask him or her to give you a certain number of them. Children who do not yet know the meaning of the number word you say may give you a handful of them, or perhaps the whole pile (Wynn, 1990, 1992).

Learning the meanings of number words takes a long time to master. According to researchers, children learn the meanings of number words *in order*. First they learn the meaning of "one." Months later they will learn "two," and still months later, they learn "three." Once children have mastered the meanings of the number words up to about "four" or "five," they begin to figure out a general rule that connects their meanings to *counting*. That is, they learn that when you count objects in a set, the last number word you say is the one that tells you how many objects there are. This is called the "cardinal principle" of counting.

Once children know the cardinal principle, they will be able to interpret the meaning of the numbers in their count list. The child knows, "If you ask me for eight objects, all I have to do is count out objects, saying one number word for each, until I get to the number eight." Children may still make errors, but these will likely be due to problems with procedures (e.g., forgetting to touch an object when he says a number word, or pointing to two objects at once), or difficulty with higher number words (Davidson, Eng & Barner, 2012).

Teacher Responses

◆ *In play, children have experience with math concepts, but without the language that helps them build a more abstract picture of what they are doing, their math experiences can only go so far. Our challenge is to connect language and hands-on experiences through play.*

◆ *We do an individual screening to find out where each child is developmentally and how we can best support them. One of the activities during the screening is to take out a set of blocks and ask the student to count them and say how many there are. A number of my young three year olds said their numbers in correct order, but weren't able to correctly identify how many were there.*

The Best Type of Math Talk

The researchers next explored whether any particular *kind* of talk about numbers was more helpful than other kinds; in other words, what kinds of math talk benefit children the most? To investigate this question, they used the same data they had collected in the above study, but this time they categorized parents' number talk into different types, and then looked at which types were most strongly linked to children's math skills.

One type of math talk that they found was important was using number words to refer to objects that were present during the interaction. This included counting out or referring to a number of visible objects, such as toys or pictures in a book. The researchers found that this type of situation was more helpful to children's learning than number talk referring to objects not present or visible (e.g., stuffed animals in another room) or "rote counting" such as counting to 10 in a game of "hide and seek."

The researchers speculate that the importance of "present objects" relates to the connection children must make between counting and understanding "how many" objects are in a set. For children to do well at the Point to X task, they must know what educational researchers call the "cardinal principle" (see Concept Box 1.2)—that the last number word you say when you count a set tells *how many* objects there are. Children learn this principle by making the connection between the counting process and the idea of "how many." They can make this connection more easily if there are actually objects present to count. For example, if an adult says, "We need five napkins," and then shows a child how to count them out ("Look, . . . one, two, three, four, five"), the child can see that the last number the adult said when counting is the same number that the adult labeled the set ("five napkins"). They can then connect the counting procedure to the word that tells them "how many."

On the other hand, if the adult counts to 10 in a game of "hide and seek," he is not actually counting objects: there isn't "10" of anything (except counting words, marking time!). Therefore there is not a clear opportunity for the child to connect the counting to "how many." This type of counting (often called "rote counting") is not useless to children: it does help them to learn the counting *sequence*. However, according to Levine's research, it is not as helpful to children's understanding of the meanings of the number words.

Levine says, "Some parents do a lot of rote counting. I have a video of a mom throwing a little girl in the air, [going] 'one, two, three, wheeeee!' Up and down. They do that maybe five times. It is a very nice interaction, and they are both having fun. The kid heard a lot of number words during that short period of time: she heard 'one,' 'two,' and 'three' over and over again. But when you think about it, what could she get out of that, other than practice with the count sequence, which she probably already knew?" According to Levine's findings, the child would probably learn more by observing counting that is related to visible objects.

Teacher Responses

◆ *I'm not surprised that math language at home would make a big difference. I wonder what it is that we could do to promote math language in the home. I feel as though not all families may know how important this is. How can we advocate for this?*

◆ *I feel that using number in concrete ways in the moment, with the child, is critical to helping him or her develop a solid understanding. I also think that they need to have exposure in a variety of concrete ways daily in order to integrate these skills.*

Concept Box 1.3   Beyond Number Talk: The Importance of Spatial Language

Levine and colleagues have found that number talk is not the only type of mathematical talk that helps children. They have also found that early experience with spatial words—like words describing shapes (square, circle, rectangle, triangle), words describing spatial features (e.g., "pointy" and "curved"), and words describing spatial relationships (e.g., "taller" and "shorter,")—is linked to performance on problems involving spatial reasoning. The more children heard spatial words between one and four years of age, the more they used spatial words, and the better they performed at spatial tasks when they were four-and-a-half years old. The spatial tasks required interpreting and analyzing objects in space, such as imagining how two triangles would look if they were rotated and then joined together, or seeing a picture of two circles stacked on top of each other, and finding this same "stacking" relationship in another picture (e.g., using hexagons instead of circles).

Levine conjectures that "[talking] about the spatial world helps kids think spatially. It promotes their thinking about the spatial world." She and her colleagues hypothesize that having the relevant vocabulary may help children to focus on spatial information (e.g., the "pointy" part), and talk themselves through the steps of a spatial problem. Knowing spatial words may also encourage children to notice spatial relationships as they go about their daily activities.

Why is spatial reasoning important? Spatial thinking is necessary for all kinds of real world tasks—for example, following a map, interpreting a graph, or even planning a block construction. Research also shows that spatial ability is connected to achievement in math and science. The stronger students' spatial abilities, the more likely they are to do well at math and science, including choosing a math or science field as a college major or career path. This holds true even when equating for mathematical and verbal abilities.

Conclusion

Levine's research suggests that language and math skills are strongly connected: the math-related language that children hear and build into their own vocabularies helps them make sense of their mathematical world. Her research also calls attention to the vast differences there are in the amount of mathematical language that children hear from parents and teachers, and how these differences impact children's developing math skills. Because other studies have shown that children from low-SES families tend to hear less language overall than their more economically advantaged peers, this work suggests that the achievement gap in math between low-and middle-income children may, at least in part, be related to the differences in their experiences with language, and in particular math-related language.

Teacher Responses
♦ *My background is with English language learners, so language is always a focus. Whenever I am teaching, I always have to be very conscious about being specific, using as much specific language as possible. But I never made connections to how important that was in academic ways. I mean, I knew it was important because I could help them acquire language, but I never connected it to other academic content like math.*

Teachers Respond to the Research

Most teachers in our seminar group were not surprised by these findings; the results made sense to them overall. In their experience, promoting language development had always been an important goal of their teaching. However, for many teachers in our group, the connection between math and language had not always been apparent: one teacher said that if you had asked her before she learned about this research about the relationship between math and language skills, she would have said that they were "[t]wo different things: math is math and language is language." For many teachers, the ideas in this chapter made them think more carefully about their own use of language in their classrooms, specifically math-related language.

The group raised several important points in response to the research and its implications for classroom practices. We describe these below, followed by Susan Levine's responses.

Language Versus Experience

One teacher wondered to what extent math-related language is *causing* children's conceptual understanding to develop, or whether learning is actually triggered by *the experiences that accompany the language*. She points out, "If you're using numbers, then you're counting stairs as you walk up the stairs, or you're pointing to the numbers on the wall: you're connecting an experience to that language. If you're not using that language, then you're probably not having that experience either." She goes on to say, "I would think they would need more than just hearing the language and words to get those concepts." This gets at an important question regarding the *underlying mechanism* for the effects we see of language on math learning. In other words, **What is actually causing the learning? Is it the language or the experiences within which the children hear the language?**

Susan Levine's Response

When we brought this question to Levine, she agreed that language and experience usually occur together, and said that because they are difficult to separate in the "real world," it is difficult to determine whether one has more influence than another. However, she said that when these have been separated in a lab setting, there is evidence that each element contributes to learning. For example, she pointed to the finding that when parents simply counted in a rote fashion without referring to concrete objects, less learning took place than when they referred to "present" objects, suggesting that the language without the experience is not enough: experience is important for learning. But she also said that language does seem to support mathematical thinking. For example, when children play with puzzles, the spatial language parents use appears to enhance children's spatial thinking even among children who play with puzzles. She also talked about cultures that have been shown not to have specific words for numbers greater than one or two, such as the Pirahã tribe in Brazil. She referred to a study that found that Pirahã adults are unable to succeed at number tasks involving knowledge of larger, exact numbers. In this case, the experience with sets of objects without the language of a count list is not enough: the language is necessary for learning. Thus Levine feels that both experience and language are important for developing mathematical skills and that these often go hand in hand.

Children's Versus Adults' Use of Language

Since the studies focused on adults' use of mathematical language, teachers raised the question of the importance of *children's* use of this language. They wondered how important it is to get children to use the words themselves versus just exposing them to the language. In sum, **What is the role of the math-related language that children *produce*? Do we know whether it is equally important that children use these words themselves, or is just hearing it enough?**

Susan Levine's Response

Levine noted that it is challenging to separate the effects of adults' and children's language use: a child must hear language in order to use it—and indeed, we know that the words children hear the most are the words they use the most. However, she also said that she does think it is important for children to be talking. She pointed to one of her studies that supports this theory. In the study, she and her colleagues first found that parents' spatial talk was linked to their children's later spatial abilities. However, when they conducted further analyses using the children's spatial talk, they found that the children's use of language appeared to serve as a *mechanism through which the parents' talk and the children's performance were connected*. In other words, the parents' talk seemed to influence the children's talk, which in turn influenced the children's spatial abilities. Thus it appeared that the *children's* talk was more directly linked to their spatial thinking than the parents' spatial talk.

Levine added that to help children use more mathematical language, it is important to pay attention to what they are interested in at the moment. By noticing what they are attending to and talking about, and then encouraging them to elaborate (e.g., "How many red cars are there?" when they are looking at a set of cars, or "How did you figure that out?" when they say a triangle is a square), you can build on their ideas and support their vocabulary growth.

The Role of Gesture in Children's Learning

A few teachers brought up the idea of *gesture* as it relates to learning—both children's and teachers' gestures. One pointed out the importance of gesture when communicating with young children and its particular relevance to students for whom English is a second language (ESL). She said, "Some children don't respond as well to verbal teaching and need visual [teaching] as well. Teachers certainly pick up on this and use a combination of the two." She suggested that it might be useful to examine the effects of teachers' gesture in combination with language when studying math learning. Other teachers pointed out their *students'* gestures. One remarked how she could often see that children understand numbers when they use their fingers to show "how many," even when they don't say the number word.

These comments point to the following question: **What role does gesture—on the part of both teachers and students—play in the relationship between math-related language and children's learning?**

Susan Levine's Response

Levine told us that her research indeed supports what these teachers noticed in the classroom: the use of gesture does seem to enhance learning. She said that this is true of gesture by both adults and the children themselves, and has been found in both number and spatial content areas. For example, in one study in which adults provided young children with input to support them in completing jigsaw puzzles, they found that when adults used gesture to point out spatial features of puzzle pieces (such as running a finger along a straight side while saying "straight side"), it helped much more than when they just used the words by themselves. The children seemed to need the gestures to clarify what the adults meant by the words. In another study they found that when children were shown cards that depicted sets of objects and asked what was on the card, children's gestures more accurately reflected the set size than their words. For example, for a set of three objects, the child might say "four" but correctly hold up three fingers. A subsequent study showed that children who produced these kinds of mismatches were better able to profit from instruction supporting the learning of the next number word—in this case, "three." (See also Chapter 4 of this volume for more on gesture and early math.)

Non-numeric Math Language

Teachers were interested to hear about the importance of spatial language (see Concept Box 1.3). However, they asked, **What about other types of non-numeric mathematical language? For example, do we know anything about general quantitative language like "all," "none," and "some?" Are there other types of mathematical language that are shown to be beneficial to children's math learning?**

Susan Levine's Response

Levine said that research does indicate that other types of language are related to children's mathematical thinking. She brought up the example of plural markers such as noun-verb agreement (e.g., "the boys run"; "the boy runs") and non-numeric quantifiers, such as "a," "some," and "all," and mentioned research showing that children's understanding of these markers is correlated with their number word knowledge. Other words she said are important to use are "equal," "less than," and "more than." Although not all of these mathematical terms have been studied carefully in a lab setting, research does indicate that children sometimes have difficulty with these terms, and that understanding them is necessary for solving math problems, beginning in early elementary school.

Precision of Language

Some teachers were interested in using more mathematical language in their classrooms, but were concerned about situations that might come up in which they did not know the most precise, "mathematically correct" terms to use to talk about an idea. They wondered whether it was better to use informal, potentially incorrect, language in order to convey the ideas, or better to not to talk about these ideas. In general, they asked, **How precise should the math language that teachers use be?**

Susan Levine's Response

Levine said that she thinks teachers should be as precise as possible without using words that are too esoteric. She said, "To the degree that you can, without confusing kids, try to enhance precision." She noted that children are good word learners and can pick up terms that adults might think are too advanced. She also said that adults should avoid giving children incorrect information that they will have to "unlearn" later. For example, some classroom shape posters label pictures incorrectly: they label a picture of a pizza slice a "triangle" (since it has one rounded side, it should not be labeled a triangle), or a picture of a ball a "circle" (it should be labeled a sphere). These are also great moments for discussion—children can be asked, for example, "Why is the pizza slice not a triangle?" or "What is the difference between a circle and a sphere?"

Cultural Considerations

One teacher pointed out the important relationship between culture and adult-child interactions. She questioned whether teachers should suggest that parents talk more with their children about math when this may conflict with those parents' cultural mores and heritage. She says, "Some cultures deemphasize verbal interactions between children and adults, and certainly the academic interactions that we see in many middle class American families, and other cultures see teaching purely [as belonging within] the realm of schools and teachers. For teachers to tell parents they need to work more with either the language or practice of math might go against such a culture. Is it our place to influence the way parents interact with their children in the home?" **How should we balance the wish to encourage parents to engage in more math-related conversation with the need to respect cultural differences?**

Susan Levine's Response

Levine said that while she does not want to recommend disregarding cultural customs, she *does* want children to succeed in school. She felt it was important to get the message out to all parents that using mathematical language with children will help them academically. She said, "Sometimes it's hard—when you tell people to talk [with their children], they don't know what to talk about." But sending out a clear message about the importance of mathematical language in particular "gives them something to talk about." She also said that giving them ideas about *how* they can incorporate this language into daily routines—such as when shopping, cooking (e.g., labeling amounts when baking—2 Tablespoons of sugar), or walking to school (e.g., counting steps or trucks)—could be helpful. She said, "Most people, in my experience, are excited about this. Most parents want their kids to be prepared for school and to succeed academically. The trick is to find culturally respectful ways to engage parents in supporting their children's math learning by incorporating math talk and activities into their daily routines."

Teachers' Ideas for Classroom Practice

In their responses to the research, teachers had many ideas about ways to incorporate math-related language in their classrooms. Below, we present some of their thoughts, and provide some context for each.

Connect Math Language to What Children Are Currently Doing; Think Ahead About Mathematical Terms Relevant to Common Activities

- *For me, the best strategy is just to apply math language and concepts all throughout the day. I look for things that my students are already interested in and find the math there. For my students who like to play in the block area, I join them and talk about height, width, area, adding, subtracting, etc. For my students in art, I may talk about the lines in their paintings, or the amount of paint we are pouring. For my students playing in housekeeping, I can talk about size as we try on clothes, count as we set the table, use one-to-one correspondence to put items away, or measure as we use various materials. I find that this works best, because it gives them real life experiences to back up their learning.*

- *Depending on what I see that a child is working on, I pick three to five words that I will repeat at least five times during the conversation with the child. For example, if the child is working on filling and emptying containers at the water table, I might choose the words level, higher, lower, full, and empty as words that I will intentionally use to describe the child's play.*

Great teachers of young children are real artists when it comes to observing and understanding children's play, and knowing how to extend it. They know just how long to watch and wait, and by providing a question, comment, or suggestion at a key moment, they can help the play become more complex or connect it to new content and ideas that can deepen it in other ways. These extensions can tap the mathematical ideas that are truly "all around us," but that may not be obvious to a young child. Given the relationship that Levine has found between math-related language and children's mathematical thinking, it is important that teachers look for and take advantage of these opportunities.

By commenting that "I see you have picked out the *tall* block instead of the *wide* one," a teacher connects math language to something the child is already thinking about, providing a cognitive boost that may prompt the child to think about the difference between "tall" and "wide." Using hand motions in this situation to indicate height versus width may help children begin to figure out this difference. By asking a child *how many* people will be eating dinner in the housekeeping area, and suggesting "Should we *count* the babies?," a teacher demonstrates the usefulness of counting within a context that is both familiar and immediately relevant to the child. By asking a child to look at the *level* of the water in cups and decide which is *higher*, and/or which *is closer to full* the teacher is pointing out connections between water level, volume, and capacity of a container. Within these play moments, children's attention is already highly engaged by their own actions; by artfully inserting their own comments, teachers use the child's interest as a "platform" upon which to present new math-related information and ideas.

In their comments above, the teachers make clear that they have thought about specific math-related words that are related to the different play areas in their classrooms, so they are ready to find ways to use them as moments arise. They also demonstrate that they have thought about the mathematical *ideas* present in these areas. As Levine's research suggests, some math talk is more valuable than others: it is not enough to simply insert as many math words as possible into a conversation (such as by counting by rote over and over again), but to use them to describe situations and problems in ways that make important distinctions (e.g., wide versus high) that are interesting and relevant to the child.

In a kindergarten classroom, where word walls are common, it may make sense to post math-related words. These could even be placed near the relevant area of the classroom (e.g., "wide" and "tall" near the block area). This can serve both to remind the teacher to use math-related language and to help children become aware of these "math words" as having discrete and important meanings. A word of caution, however, is that the words one prepares to use may not end up being the most appropriate or precise words for the situation at hand. There will always be times when teachers must think on their feet to explain unanticipated ideas that children bring up. Still, it is helpful to think ahead about language and ideas relevant to common activities in the classroom.

Connect Math to Individual Children's Interests

I had a student, age four, who had a terrible time with counting. He could rote count, but he had a weak sense of one-to-one correspondence and no cardinality beyond three. One day I brought jump ropes outside for the first time. He had never jumped rope before, but as soon as he picked one up he was able to do it. Every day he jumped rope. We started counting how many times he could jump. I could see the light bulb go on over his head as he seemed to realize that the higher the number, the longer he was jumping. When we worked with him on counting inside, he got it! He understood that the last number counted was how many when we compared what he was counting to his jumping rope! We still needed to work with him on this skill, but it was a huge breakthrough.

Early childhood classrooms have the advantage of being designed to allow the very best kind of "differentiation." When class sizes are kept small, and children are encouraged to choose their own activities, it is easier to see the strengths of each child. Early childhood teachers understand the power of building on children's strengths and allowing time for them to develop. In the example above, by connecting counting (something that was difficult for a child) with jumping rope (something that came easily to him) the teacher provided a route to understanding. The child was able to understand a key idea of counting: that the *higher* the number word, the *more* items in the set (in this case, the more jumps he completed, and the longer he jumped). The counting words were much more meaningful to him once he connected it to something he cared about.

Pair Meaningful Counting With Visual Representations of Quantity

One thing that I have done with children is, during fish feeding, to let children know that our fish requires five pieces of food. I put a random number of pieces of food in my hand, ask the child to count, and then ask if we need to add more food or take away food in order to make five pieces. For some of my oldest children this is a fairly straightforward task. But it is very difficult for many children. I will add or take away pieces for a long time with a child until we figure out the right number. However, I have begun to think that the concept of five is too abstract. And my plan, once I get fish into my classroom again, is to have a picture of five pieces of food. Hopefully this will give the children a visual representation that they can imitate to get five and make the idea easier to understand for the majority of children in my classroom.

Many early childhood classrooms have "number posters" on their wall somewhere: large-size numerals are often presented in order, generally from 1 to 10. This kind of representation is useful for familiarizing children with what the numerals look like, and may support their awareness that there is a standard sequence, but there is often no information about cardinal amount, or quantity. As Levine's research points out, cardinal meaning ("how many" a number word indicates) is a central concept in early math, and visual representations of quantities play an important role in helping children develop this understanding.

In the "fish feeding" example above, the teacher used concrete objects to help children understand the cardinal meaning of the number word "five." This is a terrific task for several reasons. First, feeding fish is a very meaningful (and interesting!) activity: children can understand why giving the fish an *exact* number of pieces is important (too few pieces will cause the fish to be hungry, while too many might make it sick). Second, five is an important "friendly number" that children need to get very comfortable with; being familiar with five will help in understanding ten. Third, because the activity is conducted with children on an individual basis, it gives the teacher a lot of information about each child's abilities to count to five and about his or her understanding of "five-ness." In essence, the activity is a mini-formative assessment. From this activity, the teacher learned that the task was too difficult for some of her younger students, and she was able to brainstorm ways to help them.

A visual representation of five, such as dots on a card, or a more literal picture of five pieces of fish food, is an excellent way to scaffold this activity. If children can place one piece of fish food on each dot or "piece" on the card, the task becomes something the teacher's youngest students can accomplish with a lot less assistance from her. This change to the activity may reduce the amount of good formative assessment information it provides, but it might also help children who need it to build an understanding of "five-ness." Adding this kind of visual representation to accompany each of the numerals on our "number poster" above could make a big difference to what children are able to learn from it. Gradually these supports can be removed as children gain an understanding of what "five" means.

Encourage Children to Explain Their Thinking

One strategy that I have found particularly helpful in developing mathematical language is asking children, "How do you know that?" Having them explain what they did or how they arrived at an answer has been very helpful for me in assessing what they know and also in providing a scaffold for defining and explaining mathematical operations. It allows me to start where they are (in their own words) and expand upon their language levels to help take them one step farther.

Asking children to justify what they are thinking by asking, "How did you figure that out?," "Why do you think that?," or "How do you know for sure?" is powerful teaching at its best. As the teacher quoted above points out, it provides her with very rich information about what children understand. This allows her to adapt her teaching to build on children's current thinking and skills while helping them continue to develop their understanding. It also, as she says, provides her with information about their abilities to express their understanding, and allows her to help them do so more precisely. For example, a child might talk about why he chose a "big" block to support a structure, when he means "tall." She can build on this, starting, as she says, with the child's language ("big") and then adding more sophisticated and precise language ("tall").

The exercise of asking a child to explain his or her thinking also provides children with practice in using math-related language *themselves*. We know from Levine's work and other literature on learning that many of us learn best when we have opportunities to talk about our thinking. Having to find the right words to match our understanding and then use them in a coherent explanation helps us to crystalize our ideas and recognize aspects that we may be confused about. Listening to and assessing the response of a conversation partner may allow us to make further connections. Thus talking about mathematical ideas is a much more active, involved experience of math language than simply hearing it from a teacher.

The Practice Standards of the Common Core State Standards for Mathematics emphasize the importance of this skill. They specify that for children to understand the math they are learning they need opportunities to "make viable arguments (about math) and critique the reasoning of others." Elementary and high school teachers who are trying to implement this practice standard are now often asking their students—some for the first time—"How do you know?" or "How did you figure that out?" Student discourse is thus becoming an important component of math class across grade levels. Providing children with practice talking about math during early education experiences will make it easier for them to participate in and gain from these discussions in later grades. And while it is often difficult for very young children to explain their thinking, it is also becoming clear that asking them to do so, and supporting them in the process, may be key to their developing understanding in all topics, and certainly in math.

Include Math Language Throughout Your Day and Routines

◆ *We do a daily attendance count to figure out how many children are at school so that children have the opportunity to count up to 20. Most of the children by January understand that the last number counted is how many we have, even if they don't always know the correct order to count.*

◆ *Our circle time learning is always centered around our leader's name. A child's name is something that is personal and very important to them. We count the letters in the leader's name, I write the number under each letter, draw the number in dots or shapes, we count again using our fingers, and then finally we use numbered blocks.*

Routines can be powerful learning opportunities, especially for mathematics. In the attendance count example above, children participate in a meaningful counting activity that provides ongoing practice with the rules of counting. The sequence of the number words, the requirement that one number word is assigned to each child, and the use of the last number word counted to name the quantity of the set are repeated consistently, day after day. In contrast, the order in which children are counted may change from day-to-day, as will the total number of children counted, depending upon attendance. Humans use clues about what is the same and what is different to construct all their knowledge, and routines are a natural structure for highlighting these things. By seeing the similarities and differences in the attendance counting process from day to day, children build an understanding of what it is that makes the counting system work.

Routines can support your use of math language in other ways as well, of course. Making a habit of having children help to set the table for snack by having them "bring four cups and four plates" means there will be many opportunities for meaningful counting over the course of a school year. Similarly, children can be prompted to action using interesting categories, as in, "All children with red in their shirts line up now . . . All children with white in their shirts line up now," helping them think about sets (such as the set of children with red in their shirts) and how they work. Early childhood classrooms are typically full of routines that help structure the day and make sure that everyone is fed, comfortable, and treated fairly. When you incorporate math into these routines, it becomes easy to use more math language every day, even without much planning.

Consider Audiotaping Yourself

Two years ago I participated in a math (PD) cohort through work. In this, we discussed how important it is to use mathematical language with young children and how this can give them new vocabulary and elevate their learning. The coordinator of the program came out and recorded a sample of me playing in the block area with two students. Afterward, he listened to this and graphed out the amount of math words that I had used. This made me realize how little math talk I was doing—and how repetitive my language was! We also talked about using really specific words when you're describing something rather than just saying words like "that," "this," "there." I realized I use those words all the time, when I could have said, "that arched block," "that triangular block," "the small block." I was just using all those empty filler words that weren't doing anything. This was my turning point: when I started to change my language in the classroom. By the end of the cohort, he came out and recorded me again. My math language doubled or tripled. Since then, I've concentrated on math language all throughout the day with my preschoolers. I can hear it making a difference in how they talk and reason. Students will be pouring milk for each other and talk about a quarter or a half a glass. When there's only a little bit of snack left, they ask me if they can count and divide it up. And this is only the math they use during mealtimes! In so many ways, I see the math language that I use resonating with them. I still feel like it takes a lot of effort to do this as a teacher, and that I still have a long way to go, but at least it's something that's more on my mind that I'm working towards.

It can be very difficult to change your teaching practice, even if you want to. Running a safe, pleasant classroom for 18–30 young children is challenging enough, let alone trying to develop their mathematical thinking. A coach or mentor can be a lot of help, since conversation about your teaching practice can increase awareness of your techniques and generate ideas on how to improve your practice, but many teachers don't have the luxury of that kind of support.

The teacher's experience described above provides a clear example of the power of self-reflection for changing practice, and suggests a possible means to this end: audiotape. If changing what you talk about and how often you do it is your goal, it stands to reason that *knowing* how you normally speak as you teach is a good first step. With or without a coach or supportive supervisor, you can audiotape yourself as you talk with children throughout the day. Audiotaping alone, however, will not do the trick: you will have to analyze your classroom talk for math-related language, counting the instances in which you use math language and looking for times when you could use language more or use it differently.

One notable aspect of the teacher's experience was that it centered on one area (the block area). Whether you audiotape yourself or not, focusing on increasing math language in one area at a time may make the process more manageable. It also may help you to think more deeply about different topics (e.g., What mathematical ideas are present in the dramatic play area? What language can I use to support these ideas?), instead of trying to think about too many topics at once.

At the end of this chapter, we have provided a list of types of math-related language you might want to look for, with some examples of each kind.

The Bottom Line

The first takeaway from this chapter is that talking about the math in the world around us is a good way to help young children begin to think mathematically. It is wonderful to see such clear evidence that what teachers and caregivers do makes a real difference in the cognitive development of young children. That is, early childhood teaching does not have to focus exclusively on social-emotional development: adults who intentionally discuss mathematics as it occurs in the child's environment foster better mathematical understanding. The care and teaching of young children, then, goes far beyond "babysitting," suggesting the importance of knowledgeable and thoughtful choices on the part of teachers. The math does not have to be complex, however. By noticing and commenting on quantity, shape, and size, and asking children to explain their own thinking on these topics, preschool teachers and other care providers can have an enormous impact.

The second takeaway is that not all children get enough opportunities to hear and use math-related language with the adults in their life, so what early childhood teachers say really matters.

All children can benefit from rich math language in the preschool environment, especially those who experience little of this language in the home environment. Without an adult to supply the words that can name things from a mathematical perspective, such children arrive at school already at a disadvantage relative to their peers. Counting the stairs as you go up, talking about the height of your block tower, and noticing that a window and a door both are rectangular shapes are the kinds of experiences children are unlikely to have on their own, but certainly are ready to learn from. As teachers and caregivers, we have an obligation to be sure that all young children hear, use, and learn the common language of mathematics, so they can enter kindergarten with the foundational knowledge that will help them think mathematically in elementary school and beyond, and that will prepare them for twenty-first century careers.

Key Research Studies Discussed

Davidson, K., Eng, K., & Barner, D. (2012). Does learning to count involve a semantic induction? *Cognition, 123*(1), 162–173.

Gunderson, E. A., and Levine, S. C. (2011). Some types of parent number talk count more than others: Relations between parents' input and children's cardinal-number knowledge. *Developmental Science, 14*(5), 1021–1032.

Jordan, N. C., Huttenlocher, J., and Levine, S. C. (1994). Assessing early arithmetic abilities: Effects of verbal and nonverbal response types on the calculation performance of middle-and low-income children. *Learning and Individual Differences, 6*(4), 413–432.

Klibanoff, R. S., Levine, S. C., Huttenlocher, J., Vasilyeva, M., and Hedges, L. V. (2006). Preschool children's mathematical knowledge: The effect of teacher "math talk." *Developmental Psychology, 42*(1), 59.

Levine, S. C., Suriyakham, L. W., Rowe, M. L., Huttenlocher, J., and Gunderson, E. A. (2010). What counts in the development of young children's number knowledge? *Developmental Psychology*, 46(5), 1309.

Pruden, S. M., Levine, S. C., and Huttenlocher, J. (2011). Children's spatial thinking: Does talk about the spatial world matter? *Developmental Science*, 14(6), 1417–1430.

Wynn, K. (1990). Children's understanding of counting. *Cognition*, 36(2), 155–193.

Wynn, K. (1992). Children's acquisition of the number words and the counting system. *Cognitive Psychology*, 24(2), 220–251.

Resource: Sample Math-Related Language

Cardinal Amount Words
- One, two, three, ten, etc. (especially to name the amount of a set with objects/images present)
- Pair (as in mittens), trio

Non-specific Amount and Comparison Words
- All, some, none
- More, less, fewer, equal

Words About Position
- First, second, third
- Next to
- In front of, behind, under, above
- Last

Words About Shapes
- Rectangle, triangle, circle, square, oval
- Cube, sphere, prism, pyramid, cone
- Straight, curved, flat
- Edge, corner, surface

Words That Describe Spaces and Objects
- Deep, shallow
- Narrow, thin, wide, thick
- Tall, short

Names of Measurable Attributes
- Length, width, depth (long, wide, deep)
- Weight, height

2

The Role of Adult and Environmental Input in Children's Math Learning

Donna Johnson and Lisa Ginet, with Kelly Mix

Parents are children's first teachers. Most parents take that role very seriously and want to do all they can to encourage their child's success in school and life. Early childhood teachers also know that the early years are important years for learning and want to do their best to support the development of young children. To help support children, parents and teachers provide them with various types of what psychologists call "input," by talking to them and making sure they have experiences with books and toys. But, the question is, how much does the *type* of input matter?

For this chapter, we interviewed Kelly Mix, a cognitive psychologist and a professor at the University of Maryland. Mix started her career as an elementary school teacher and was intrigued by the cognitive processes that take place as children are learning. She decided to pursue a graduate degree so that she could study the specific mechanisms by which children learn mathematics, and how teacher and parent input can support this learning. In this chapter, we will look at three of her studies that explore types of input that help children acquire mathematical concepts and improve in mathematics skills.

What the Research Says

The Role of Specific Types of One-to-One Play in Learning Numerical Equivalence

This group has four bears and the other group has four cars. They both have the same number. How do children develop the idea of numerical equivalence—that two sets have the same quantity? Usually, when we think about comparing sets, we are thinking about other attributes of those sets. Color, size, and type of object are all features of the sets that we can compare. How do children learn to compare the *numerical* attribute of sets—that is, see what a set of four bears and a set of four cars have in common? This was the question that Mix and colleagues investigated in the first study we explore.

Mix's work was influenced by the ideas of Northwestern University psychologist Dedre Gentner, who studies the way that children and adults use comparisons between objects or ideas to develop new ideas—a process that she calls "structure mapping." Structure mapping begins when just one similarity is noticed between the entities being compared. Noticing this one similarity leads the learner to align the objects or ideas, "mapping" the common features from one entity to the other. As more features are mapped, more similarities are sought, and the more likely it is that any common features that exist between the entities will emerge. So, the more similarities that exist between two entities, the more likely it is that people will begin to compare them and see whatever *other* commonalities they have—such as the fact that two sets have the same quantity of members.

Mix wondered if this structure mapping process would be useful in supporting children's recognition of numerical equivalence. In order to test this, Mix needed to set up a situation that would prompt children to make a comparison—to begin the structural alignment process so that quantity as an attribute might be revealed. In considering the various contexts that could cause children to pair objects across sets, Mix asked whether aligning sets of objects so that there are similarities in their spatial arrangement would lead children to compare them numerically, either by counting each set or using one-to-one correspondence.

There are many situations in everyday play where two sets of objects are spatially paired together and comparisons can be made. For example, when children help at snack time, they might pair objects (set out one napkin for each chair at the table) or distribute objects (give out one cookie to each child). In the years preceding this study, Mix had carefully observed and recorded her son, from the ages of 12 to 38 months, engaging in different types of one-to-one correspondence activities. She noticed that one type of activity occurred *just before* he developed numerical equivalence. The activity involved placing loose objects into a container with slots, such as putting eggs into an egg carton or balls into a muffin tin. This made her wonder whether putting objects into containers—an activity she called "objects-with-slots"—could be a powerful context for surfacing the idea of numerical equivalence.

Why might these spatial alignment activities—more than setting the table or handing out cookies—help children to develop an understanding of numerical equivalence? Mix's idea was that "objects-with-slots" activities make the attribute of number visually apparent: the numerical equivalence of the two sets is visible as the slots are being filled. If there is an open slot or there are extra objects to insert, the question of "how many more/less" surfaces very quickly. In other activities, such as distributing objects to people, it is harder to see how the two groups align. In Mix's words, "If children hand out cookies to a playgroup, the sets will be moving. One set will be eating the other." This is clearly not a useful context for comparing quantities!

Concept Box 2.1   One-to-One Correspondence

One-to-one correspondence is a relationship that exists between two sets of objects. When counting, it is the relationship between the set of number names and the set of objects being counted, where one number is named for each object counted. When thinking about two sets of objects, one-to-one correspondence means that for every item in one set, there is a corresponding item in the other set. When there is one-to-one correspondence between two sets of objects, there is also numerical equivalence—the two sets have the same number of objects in them.

In this study, Mix wanted to see if exposure to more focused one-to-one correspondence (objects-with-slots) activities would help children think about how two sets are related numerically. To test this, Mix and her colleagues used a task called the "cross mapping task" that assessed whether children can match sets based only on their quantities. In the task, children were first given a target card showing a set of objects, and then were asked to select, from a choice of three cards, the one that "matched" the target card. Three types of cards were always given as choices (see Figure 2.1). One had the same quantity but different objects than the target card. Another showed the same objects but a different quantity than the target card. A third showed a different quantity and different object than the target card. Before starting the test trials, children were given several training trials in which they were shown that the card that "matched" was the one with the same quantity. This is a difficult task for children because they have to overcome the inclination to select the card with the same object on it. Previous studies had shown that children do not typically succeed on this task until around age four.

The researchers tested 37 three year olds with this task. They then excluded from the study the children who performed above "chance" level (above the level they would reach if they were randomly guessing—in this case, 33% correct), since these children might understand numerical equivalence already. This left 30 three-year-olds.

Next, the researchers divided the children randomly into two groups. Both groups of children were given three sets of toys to take home every two weeks (see Figure 2.2). One group of children was

Figure 2.1 Cross-mapping task

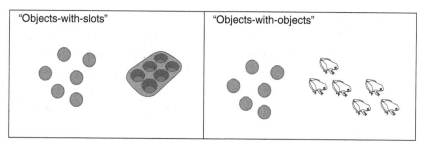

Figure 2.2 Examples of toy sets

given "objects-with-slots" sets: these were sets that included a group of objects and a container with an equivalent number of slots or openings (e.g., six whiffle balls and a muffin tin with six spaces). The other group was given "objects-with-*objects*" sets. They included two groups of objects that were equivalent in number but had no other obvious connection (e.g., six whiffle balls and six toy frogs). Parents were told to make the toys available for the children to play with at all times, and they were asked to keep logs that recorded how, and how often, the children played with the sets of toys. They kept each set of toys for two weeks, for a total of six weeks of play. At the conclusion of the six weeks, the children were tested again on numerical equivalence using the cross-mapping task.

The researchers found that while both groups of children performed better on the task after playing with the toys, the group that played with the objects-with-slots sets showed greater improvement. In addition, many more of the children in the objects-with-slots group performed above chance level (more than 33% of items correct). This suggested that these children were better able to understand numerical equivalence.

The parent logs also revealed interesting information. The children in both groups played with the toys for about the same amount of time, but the difference was in *how* the children played with the toys. The children in the objects-with-slots group frequently played with both groups of toys, creating play situations where they were putting the objects in and out of the slots (like making cupcakes), while the objects-with-objects group frequently played with the two groups of toys separately. Thus, it seemed that Mix's hypothesis was correct— that the objects-with-slots toys encouraged children to play with the toys such that the two sets aligned.

This study suggests that type of input matters in helping children construct mathematical concepts. Specifically, providing materials that encourage children to make quantitative comparisons between sets (objects-with-slots) may help young children construct the understanding of numerical equivalence between sets of objects. Mix argues that the objects-with-slots sets "ground the idea of number and numerical equivalence for them in a physical model."

Teacher Responses

◆ *It makes sense that the objects-with-slots sets help the children. As students put one item into each slot, they can visually see that the sets are either the same or not. This would be more difficult in the objects-with-objects sets because, for example, three bears look so different from three cars, and without the slots, it's harder to make the one-to-one relationships between them clear.*

◆ *I like that Mix pointed out that the attribute of number has to be visually apparent (as in the objects-with-slots sets). This made me think about math tools like 10-frames, which are essentially rectangles made up of 10 squares organized in two parallel rows of five. Sometimes we have children fill 10-frames with objects, so that the squares are really acting as "slots."*

Acquisition of the Cardinal Word Principle: The Role of Labeling and Counting as Input

In the next study, Mix and her colleagues investigated how certain kinds of input might help children learn another important mathematical concept: the cardinal word principle. The cardinal word principle states that the last word in a count represents the quantity of the set (see Figure 2.3). In other words, when counting a set of objects, the last number word you say tells you how many objects are in the set (for further information on this idea, see Concept Boxes 1.1 and 1.2 in Chapter 1 of this book). In this way, learning to count means learning to think about number words in two ways simultaneously, both as markers in a count sequence and as words that describe a total quantity. So how do children discover that the last word in a count stands for its cardinality?

Much research suggests that children must experience an overlap between counting and cardinality to signal that the two ideas are

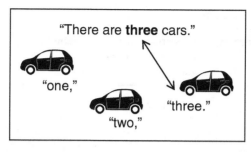

Figure 2.3 Mapping the cardinal label to the number words used in the counting process

related. Small sets may be ideal for this because children can recognize and name the quantity of small sets without counting (by subitizing, or automatically "seeing" how many there are). If they can count the small set ("one, two, three") and they also know the cardinality (three) by subitizing, perhaps the overlap in number words is enough of a connection to link counting and cardinality.

In this study, Mix again wondered if facilitating structure mapping would help children acquire the cardinal principle. Recall that in structure mapping, people detect similarities between objects or ideas, and the more comparisons they make, the more likely it is that less obvious relationships surface. So, if children notice that there are shared number words used in counting a set and in naming the cardinality of the set, they might wonder how else these sets (set of number words and set of objects being counted) are the same. Mix wondered whether certain kinds of input would better support children to see the *similarity* in the word but the *difference* in its use to make the connection between counting and cardinality—in other words, whether children would understand that "three" can represent the quantity of fingers on one hand *and* the word that comes between "two" and "four" when counting.

Mix investigated this question with two experiments. In the first experiment, children received training once a week for six weeks involving picture books that displayed sets of objects (e.g., three crackers or four ducks). Sixty 3½ year olds participated in the study. Children were randomly assigned to one of five conditions that either aligned or did not align cardinality and counting, as described in Table 2.1. That is, sometimes they heard number words used to count but not to describe a total amount, sometimes they heard number words used to

Table 2.1 Training conditions

Condition	Counting	Labeling quantity (cardinality) of the set	Example
Comparison	✓	✓	"Look, this page has three crackers. Can you say it with me? Three crackers. Let's count them, one, two, three!"
Counting	✓	✗	"Look, this page has crackers. Let's count them together: 'one (pointing to object), two (pointing to object), three (pointing to object).'"
Naming	✗	✓	"Look: this page has three crackers. Can you say it with me? Three crackers."
Alternating	Alternated across sessions		This group alternated the type of training session—counting the sets one week and then naming the sets the next week.
Control	✗	✗	"This page has crackers. They are yummy. Can you say it with me? Yummy."

describe a total amount but not to count, and other times they heard both uses, with both directed toward the same set of objects.

To test children's learning, researchers tested them three times: before the first training session, immediately following the third training session, and immediately following the sixth training session. In each testing period, they tested children on various counting skills, including one intended to measure their understanding of the cardinal principle (asking children to produce, from a pile, a certain number of objects).

The researchers found that only children in the Comparison condition improved on these tasks. In fact, after three weeks of training in the Comparison condition, children demonstrated an understanding of the cardinal word principle, but even six weeks of training with the other conditions was not sufficient. This study suggested that labeling the cardinality and then immediately counting a variety of sets helped children to connect counting and cardinality, whereas providing the same amounts of counting or labeling alone did not help. In other words, providing a structure that helped children map the cardinal label to the last number word counted helped children learn the cardinal principle.

Next, Mix and her colleagues asked what kinds of input parents typically give to children regarding number. Parents were videotaped as they read two trade books to their preschool children—one that was about number and one that was not. Parent language was then coded to determine how often they specifically provided input that included both the cardinal label as well as counting. Results of this experiment indicated that the parents almost always read the text of the book, regardless of the book's content. When parents elaborated on the book, they commented on non-numerical information much more frequently than they did on numerical information. Even when they did elaborate on the numerical information, the number of times that they labeled the quantity of the set and then counted the set was small (only once out of 79 utterances), even when using a book about number.

Typically, it takes children about 18 months to acquire the cardinal word principle, if measured from the time they start learning the counting sequence. This study showed that after experiencing labeling and counting of the same sets in close time proximity, children developed cardinal understanding at a faster pace: "Label + count" training (the Comparison condition) improved children's understanding of cardinality after only three sessions. The findings seem to indicate that children can acquire the cardinal word principle more quickly if the right type of input is provided. At the same time, the typical input provided by parents is not input that is going to support a deeper understanding of the cardinal word principle.

The Effect of Spatial Training on Children's Mathematical Ability

In the two studies above, Mix examined the ways that children create connections between mathematical concepts, and what kinds of input might support those connections. In her more recent work, as she told us, she takes a step back to think about what mechanisms children use to make these sorts of connections, and whether at least some of them are *spatial* in nature. If they are, it is possible that training on spatial thinking could improve math performance.

Spatial thinking involves perceiving objects in space, thinking about how they relate to one another and to the viewer, and visualizing how they might look when turned or moved. Many studies have demonstrated that people who are good at spatial tasks also do well in mathematics. After thoroughly reviewing the research literature about the connection between spatial and math tasks, Mix and her colleague Yi-Ling Cheng found a firm basis to conclude that the two types of tasks share cognitive processes, and that the connection is apparent as early as preschool. In other words, even at a very young age, children who are better at spatial thinking perform better in math. Their next question was whether training children on spatial tasks can improve their performance on math tasks.

To test this, Mix and Cheng recruited 58 six-to eight-year-old children to participate in a study. First, they gave the children a math pre-test. This included single-digit number fact problems (e.g., 4 + 5 = __), two- and three-digit calculation problems (56–6 = __; 124 + 224 = __), and missing term problems (4 + __ = 12). There were both addition and subtraction problems within the three problem types.

Next, they randomly divided the children into two groups: a spatial training group and a control group. The spatial training involved a 40-minute session focused on mental rotation. Children saw two shapes and then were asked to find, out of four choices, a bigger shape that could be made when the two smaller shapes were rotated and combined (see Figure 2.4). After making their selection, the children were given the two smaller shapes on separate pieces of cardstock, and they were able put the two pieces together, either confirming their choice or indicating what the correct choice was. Children in the control group worked on crossword puzzles during the 40-minute session. After the training session, they completed the same test that they did before the training.

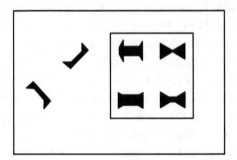

Figure 2.4 Sample mental rotation training item

The researchers found that the children in the spatial training group improved significantly more than the control group on the math test. In other words, spatial training seemed to help students with non-spatial math tasks. Why would this be? To investigate further, the researchers looked at performance on the three types of problems separately. They found that the type of problem that the spatial training group improved the most on was the missing-term problems (e.g., $4 + \_\_ = 12$). The researchers could not explain with confidence *how* the training may have helped the children. One suggestion was that perhaps the training helped the children to solve the problems by mentally rotating them to a more conventional form (e.g. $4 + \_\_ = 12$ becomes $12 - 4 = \_\_$).

Mix is still exploring the underlying processes that connect spatial ability and other non-spatial math skills. She recognizes that more needs to be done to understand the connection, and how it might be leveraged by educators. However, this study was the first to show a direct effect of spatial training on math performance, and that certain types of problems are impacted more than others. Mix says, "The work is still emerging and somewhat controversial, but I think it's a direction worth pursuing."

Teacher Responses

◆ *I have observed that children who are strong with spatial reasoning, like puzzles or particular art explorations like collage, tend to have a strong foundation in numeracy, number sense, and comparing small quantities of sets.*

◆ *I can't help but wonder why there is a connection between spatial and non-spatial math thinking. I have seen a few students who excel in spatial thinking tasks, such as making elaborate pattern block pinwheels or solving highly difficult pattern block puzzles, but who struggle terribly in other mathematical skills, such as counting or number sense.*

◆ *I think spatial thinking helps children when they are learning about fractions and multiplication. The composition and decomposition of shapes and arrays are good models for equal parts.*

◆ *I think it is interesting that spatial and kinesthetic input are used so much in pre-K and Kindergarten curricula, but in grades 1 and 2—especially as students get into adding and subtracting two-digit numbers—there is a quick shift to algorithmic solutions. Then, all of a sudden, in third grade, when multiplication and fractions are introduced, there are so many more spatial representations used.*

Conclusion

Kelly Mix is interested in the cognitive processes that take place as children engage in learning. Much of her work focuses on how input—whether adult or environmental—impacts children's thinking about foundational math concepts, with particular emphasis on the role of visual-spatial and structural components of the input. The research indicates that certain types of input do seem to help children learn mathematical concepts, perhaps because they prompt children to draw critical connections.

Teachers Respond to the Research

The teachers in our group had a lively discussion about Mix's studies and their implications for classroom instruction. They had many questions about specifics of the tasks in the studies and how altering them might change the results. They also talked about ways that the input in the studies relates to materials and tasks that they use in their own classrooms. Below are some of the main themes of their discussion.

Materials That Support Children's Understanding of Numerical Equivalence

The findings of the numerical equivalence study made sense to the teachers. They were able to see why the process of physically filling the slots with the balls, rather than playing with two seemingly separate groups of toys, would encourage children to see a connection between the two sets of objects. This observation led to a discussion about what it was about the objects-with-slots sets that helped children, and what the implications might be for classroom materials. One teacher asked, "If the slots were not connected, like loose cups, would that lead children to make similar connections to numerical equivalence, or was it the structure of the slots themselves?" That is, what was it that helped the children—was it the fact that one set of objects was containers (e.g., cups) or the fact that the containers were held together as a set within the structure of the muffin tin or egg carton? They also wondered, for the objects-with-objects sets, whether the relationship between the objects mattered. For example, children didn't play with the frogs and balls together, but perhaps they would play with frogs and lily pads together because they have a relationship, even though there are no "slots" involved.

Thinking about the structure of the slots in the objects-with-slots sets made the teachers think about classroom tools that provide ways to structure quantities, such as "10-frames" (see Figure 2.5). Teachers felt that 10-frames give students a visual structure for organizing quantity and can help students think about numerical equivalence. One pre-K teacher thought that this fit with the findings of the study, given that the objects with slots provided a similar organizing visual structure for children.

The teachers wondered: **Was there something in the "slotted-ness" of the slots that supports one-to-one play? If the connection/relationship between the two sets of toys were stronger (like frogs and lily pads) or some other pairing that seemed to "go together," would that encourage one-to-one play? To what extent do visual-spatial structures used in classrooms, such as dot cards and 10-frames, help children see mathematical relationships, particularly numerical relationships like numerical equivalence?**

Kelly Mix's Response

Yes, I believe the shape of the slots and the way they invite objects to be placed was a major reason that these were more effective than loose object sets, but the ideas you've raised about conceptual connections are another great way to leverage the same mechanism. I considered doing a mommy-baby animal condition with mother animals (bear, tiger, fish) and babies that match but never did it. I bet it would work!

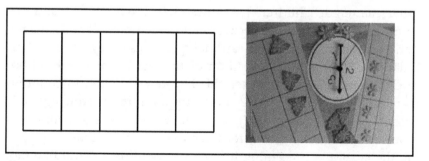

Figure 2.5 Examples of 10-frames

I agree that 10-frames, dot cards, and other spatial supports might capitalize on the same mechanism by helping children align the items in one set with the items in another. 10-frames naturally direct attention to sets of ten or tens as units, so they are well suited to helping children recognize equivalence for these larger sets. However, 10-frames don't lend themselves as well to representing and matching smaller sets because the number of slots is not equal to the number of dots, and children would need to see the equivalence of various set sizes across partially filled dot cards. This may not be so easy. Cards with sets of dots or pictures that children can match may do more to promote equivalence concepts across a range of set sizes. Probably the more these promote one-to-one correspondence, the more useful they will be. For example, the arrays on both cards might be arranged in lines that can be matched up. Alternatively, the objects themselves could invite alignment if they have meaningful one-one relations, such as children to cookies or parent animals to baby animals. Frames that have other numbers of slots, such as 3-frames or 5-frames, could also be used.

Digging Into the "Label and Count" Study

In discussing the "label and count" study, teachers had questions about why this worked and whether slight differences might have the same effect. They wondered whether the order matters when you are connecting the quantity with the count sequence. Would "count then label" have been as effective as "label then count"? In other words, **What is driving the deepening of the understanding of cardinality?**

Kelly Mix's Response

In terms of the order of counting and labeling, we found that the order mattered. Children fared best when we labeled and then counted. This made sense because children commonly miss the relation between counting and cardinality because they think the cardinal label is merely a repetition of the last count word, without cardinal meaning. You can see this if you ask a child to count and then ask them "How many?" If they respond by counting again, it's probably because they don't understand that the last count word represents the total number for the set. We thought that by separating the label and presenting it first, the count itself would be more like a proof (i.e., "I think that's four. Let's count to be sure."), so the cardinal meaning was separated. All that said, other researchers have not found a difference between these two orders (See Art Baroody's recent work), so this may be a subtle effect that only helps certain children. What we know about adult input for number, in general, is that it is relatively infrequent. Furthermore, children whose parents and teachers talk about mathematics and number more than others' also perform better on mathematics tasks. So I always tell teachers to simply increase the amount of time they spend talking about numbers and mathematics. If you do no more than increase the amount of exposure your students are getting, you're probably already having a significant impact.

Differences in the Space-Math Connection Across Children and Ages

Teachers were very interested in the connection between spatial and mathematical skills. They could think of examples of their own students that both supported and contradicted this finding. For example, while one teacher felt that the findings, in general, matched with what she had seen in her preschool classroom, another teacher could think of certain students who they felt were strong in certain spatial tasks like puzzles or pattern blocks, but seemed to struggle with mathematical skills like counting or number sense. The second teacher asked, "If there is a connection, would we potentially see a stronger association between abilities in these seemingly disparate activities?" Further, because teachers in the group teach different grade levels, they wondered whether differences in the space-math connection across children had to do with age and, relatedly, whether there is an age at which the connection between space and math skills becomes particularly important.

The teachers asked, **Why might the connection between spatial and math skills be found in some but not all students? Is there an age at which it is important to start encouraging spatial thinking?**

Kelly Mix's Response

These are great observations about individual differences. I don't think we know enough about the connection between spatial skill and mathematics to fully explain them, but my hunch is that some children are better at spontaneously recruiting spatial representations in mathematics than others. For example, some children solving a word problem might create a mental model of the problem that they move around to understand what's happening, whereas others with equally good spatial skills do not. This insight—knowing how to use spatial representations to help you understand a problem—may be something we need to teach some children. There's some interesting research by Lindsey Richland showing that when teachers use analogies in the classroom, like using an orange to teach about perimeter and volume, children need a lot of help mapping the mathematics symbols onto the model. Maybe some children need the same kind of scaffolding to create and map spatial analogies.

In terms of age groups, in a recent study, my colleagues and I compared kindergarten, third-, and sixth-grade students and found no difference in the correlation between spatial skill and mathematics. The correlation was strong, and equally so, at all three grade levels. We and others have also found spatial training effects in children as young as first grade, and longitudinal effects of preschool block play on high school mathematics achievement, so I would say it's never too early to start! It's funny because many of the activities that are turning out to be of great benefit to young children—things like block play, making patterns, completing shape puzzles—are classic early childhood activities that kids have always loved.

Visual-Spatial Experiences That Support Mathematical Thinking

The teachers saw connections between the spatial training study and the visual-spatial nature of the objects-with-slots sets in the numerical equivalence study. They could see how the visual-spatial input in each study helped support children's mathematical thinking. They thought of other examples in which visual-spatial awareness may help children in math, such as subitizing small quantities, thinking about numbers on a number line, representing solutions to math problems in more than one way, fractions, multiplication using arrays, and composing and decomposing "easy" numbers to solve two-and three-digit addition and subtraction problems. One teacher thought that spatial skills might help children in estimating quantities, such as approximating how many objects are in a jar. She commented, "If children are skilled at conducting mental rotation tasks,

I imagine that they might mentally rotate the objects in ways that help them see the entire set so that they can more accurately estimate the number in the jar."

They asked, **Are there specific math activities that benefit from strong spatial thinking? If so, why? In other words, what are the connections and mechanisms at play that connect spatial thinking and other mathematical skills?**

Kelly Mix's Response

There are trends in my studies that suggest a greater role for spatial skill in mathematics tasks that may benefit from visualization, such as word problems, and mathematics skills that are new to children. So, for example, the link between spatial processing and performance on fraction problems is greater in third grade than it is in sixth grade. We think this is because fractions are new to third grade students and these children must work harder to interpret the mathematics symbols. For sixth grade students, fractions are more familiar and children's processing may be more automatic. In this case, spatial visualization may be less helpful. However, these subtle effects emerge against the backdrop of a strong general connection between all spatial skills and all mathematics skills, so I would say any spatial experiences are likely to be of broad benefit to mathematics learning.

I think about the basic mechanism in terms of symbol grounding. How do children bring meaning to these arbitrary words and scribbles on the page? Linguist George Lakoff argued that we ground symbols in bodily movement and physical experiences in space. Building on that idea, it makes sense that children with better spatial skills would also perform better in mathematics, because they are well equipped to ground those mathematical symbols. The teachers' insights are dead on. Developing a sense of magnitude or "numbers in their head" is another way of saying "symbol grounding." I know when I was teaching mathematics, we were told that it's helpful to expose children to concrete models or pictures as a way to help them comprehend mathematics symbols. I would say it's best to go one step further, and think of symbol grounding as a necessary prerequisite, rather than a beneficial add-on. Some children will spontaneously recruit spatial metaphors to help them with symbol grounding, and others will not. This is an important leverage point for teachers.

Generalizations About the Effects of Different Types of Input on Learning

Given that information gets communicated to children all the time, teachers were intrigued by the idea that it is not just *what* is communicated, but also *how*, that matters for learning. While they could easily think of ways of providing input they have found helpful for students (see Teachers' Ideas for Classroom Practice section), they found it difficult to find commonalities among these strategies.

They wanted to know: **As we think about adult and environmental inputs that support children's mathematical understanding, are there some generalizations that can help guide a teacher in knowing what strategies to use? Are there certain types of adult input that are clearly more impactful? Given the large number of mathematical concepts that children are developing, how can you know what procedures, methods, strategies, and so on to use to best deepen children's mathematical understanding?**

Kelly Mix's Response

Here too I recall Lindsey Richland's research on the need to carefully scaffold analogies and examples. When I was a young teacher, we were simply told to expose children to concrete models, as if the connections would be so obvious children would immediately apprehend them. As teachers, we could see this wasn't happening. Now research clearly bears this out. It takes step-by-step scaffolding for learners to benefit from illustrations of all kinds. In terms of deepening children's understanding, a guiding concept is forming connections. You can think of it this way: You probably have a route you like to take to work, and if you follow that route, you will always get from point A to point B, and that's fine. That's like knowing to count 1-2-3-4 in order or memorizing 2 + 2 = 4. But what happens if there's construction and you can't take your preferred route? Ideally, you can mentally represent the roads in your town and how they are interrelated. With this map, you can imagine and plan out many alternative routes. That's the goal for mathematics too. In early childhood, this might mean helping children see that 1-2-3-4 is related to the label "4" and that this set can be decomposed into 1 + 3 or 2 + 2 and it's always the same, or that it is 1 less than 5 and 1 more than 3. Probably the most important thing teachers can do for children is help them discover all of these interconnections, rather than learning a particular strategy or problem-solving approach. A deep understanding of numerical relations will equip children with the foundation they need to invent and comprehend all kinds of problem solutions later.

Parental Support and Math Understanding

Early childhood teachers work hard to build home-school connections. The discussion of the findings from the parent portion of the "label and count" study raised a number of issues for the group. First, the teachers were reminded again of the importance of parent education, particularly about math. So much emphasis is placed on literacy and getting parents involved in reading to their children, but little is said about how or why it is important for parents to have "math conversations" with their children. This led the group to other questions: **How can they help parents understand when and how to use mathematical language to support student's mathematical understanding? As you think about the work you have done, are there suggestions that you think teachers could share with parents?**

Kelly Mix's Response

Gosh, the role of parents in developing strong mathematics skills cannot be overstated. They have so many opportunities to inject math talk into daily life and we know from research (see Susan Levine's recent studies) that children greatly benefit when parents do this. I think the important message to convey is that exposure of any kind is better than no exposure. I worry that parents avoid talking about math because they think they can't do it correctly. While there may be subtle benefits of some kinds of math talk versus others, the most important thing is to talk about math somehow, every day. Parents understand that reading to children prepares them to become readers in school. I'd love for them to think of math the same way. Just mention numbers or count when it comes up in everyday activities. Math talk doesn't have to be perfect or formal. It just has to happen. It can be playful, too. I have three teenagers, and when they were younger, they would sometimes say things about math that weren't accurate. Rather than correct them, I would try to say something like, "Oh that's interesting. You think there are more cups than bears? How can we check that?" and we'd laugh if we counted or matched up the sets and discovered there were fewer. Modeling the process of figuring things out is more important than always being correct.

Teachers' Ideas for Classroom Practice

How can teachers take what Kelly Mix and others have learned about the role of input in children's mathematical learning, and apply it to what happens in the classroom on a daily basis? As we think about adult input, the research confirms what resonates with teachers—that adult input matters a lot! Below we describe some of the ideas teachers had for being deliberate about the input they provide their students.

Provide Children With Materials That Allow Them to Make Connections

◆ *I have noticed that playing matching games with dot cards where the child has to find the dot card that has the same quantity on it but in a different formation has been very helpful for my students. I think this draws their attention to the idea that a quantity can be represented in many different formations and then allows them to see that in more natural instances in their lives.*

It is important for children to be able to make comparisons so that they can see and discover relationships that exist among objects, groups, and quantities. As the teacher quoted above noticed, certain types of materials may encourage children to make these comparisons. In the activity she describes, children see cards with dot formations of different numbers and have to find the ones with the same quantity, even if they look different (e.g., matching a card with three dots in a line and a card showing three dots in an "L" shape).

Take care when selecting materials for different activities, thinking about the different types of comparisons children might make. For example, in a sorting activity, providing objects of different colors, quantities, and sizes can help children make different kinds of comparisons: they might notice that there are a lot more red beads than blue beads, and they also might notice that a lot of beads can fit in one egg carton slot, but only one toy car can. Cards that represent the same small quantities with different pictures (e.g., dots, ladybugs, stars, lines, etc.) can help children realize that cards can match by picture type (the card with three ladybugs and the card with two ladybugs), and by quantity (the card with three ladybugs and the card with three lines). In the block area, blocks of different shapes and sizes enable children to explore the ways that varying the orientation, position, and quantity of the different blocks can produce very different kinds of towers. If provided with carefully selected materials, children can make connections and discover relationships in every area of the early childhood classroom.

Talk to Children About the Connections They See

◆ *When I first started teaching, I thought that what I had to do was set up the environment and provide the activities in order for students to learn. But my experience has taught me that I need to also be intentional about verbalizing objectives and connections.*

Although the materials that we provide to children for exploration can illuminate or hide the math, Mix reminds us that the materials in and of themselves are usually not enough: having conversations with children about their ideas is an important part of the process. For example, a teacher might ask a child *why* he thinks more beads than cars fit in the egg container. Having a conversation with children about the math they are engaging in and getting them to explain their thinking will help children make connections and see relationships. Engaging in math conversations also gives children the opportunity to consider other ways of thinking about solving a problem.

Create Authentic Contexts for Doing Math

◆ *I use books to narrate a real-life situation where one-to-one correspondence or numerical equivalence is important, such as* 10 for Dinner *by Jo Bogart or* Rooster's Off to See the World *by Eric Carle.*

◆ *I make sure to keep "naked numbers" out of the classroom. That is, I help children connect the numbers with objects that they were counting. For example, when a child says "I'm four," I say, "Oh, you're **four years old**," or when they say, "I have two!" I say, "You have **two apples**, wow!"*

Context helps children to find meaning in the problem, which in effect helps them make sense of it. All math tells a story—the symbols that we write and the equations that we solve have at the most basic level a story that connects it to real life. Ideally, there is a genuine question that we are trying to answer: a real problem that we are trying to solve. As the teachers mentioned—and Mix agreed—certain contexts, such as pairing up frogs and lily pads or mama and baby animals, could support children in exploring the concept of numerical equivalence. When the number of frogs and lily pads or mamas and babies do (or do not) line up, they might begin to think about questions like "Which group has more?" and even "How *many* more?"

Reading children's literature can provide a context for mathematical thinking and conversation to take place. After reading a book like *10 for Dinner*, an authentic opportunity exists to set the table for dinner at home or lunch at school. A very natural conversation can occur about the concept of one to one correspondence as children match the number of people to the number of cups and plates. Numerical equivalence opportunities also exist if there are not enough cups or plates for the people who are going to eat. These are only a few of the many opportunities that exist for children to experience math both at school and at home. Math is all around, and as we see it, we can help children find meaning in that math.

Help Children Nurture and Use Their Spatial Thinking and Visualization Skills

◆ *I often see children applying spatial thinking during dot card number talks, when they need to "conceptually subitize." They have to "move" or spatially "group" certain amounts together in order to figure out the quantity being represented.*

It is important not only to provide children with visual representations of quantity, such as in dot or picture cards, dominoes and dice, but also to draw their attention to the spatial structures in these representations. For example, a popular activity is to show children dot cards briefly, asking children to see if they can figure out how many dots are on the card without counting. The teacher then asks children to explain how they figured out how many dots there were. To support attention to spatial structures, a teacher might actually mark on the dot cards as children are explaining how they saw the quantity. (This can be done with wipe-off markers on laminated cards. See Concept Box 2.2.)

Concept Box 2.2　Using Spatial Structures to Explain Thinking in Dot Card Number Talks

A kindergarten teacher shows a small group of children the dot card (figure a) briefly, and then asks them how many they saw. Children shout out, "Five!" The teacher then draws the image from the card on the board and asks each child to explain how she or he knew it was five.

Child 1: "I knew it was five because I saw the four and one more." *The teacher circles four dots in the 2×2 array at the top, and then the one remaining dot on the bottom left (figure b), saying, "So she saw four on the top, and one on the bottom, and she knew that four plus one is five."*

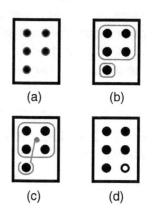

Figure 2.6 Original dot card and images that teacher draws on board

Child 2: "I saw the four, and moved the one dot to the center to look like five on a dice." *Teacher circles one dot on the bottom and draws an arrow to the center of the four dots at the top (figure c) and says, "He knew that on dice, when you see the pattern of four dots in a square and one in the middle, it's five. So she imagined moving the one from the bottom up to the middle, and knew it had to be five."*

Child 3: "This reminded me of six on a dice with one missing." *Teacher says, "You mean you saw it would be six if there was one here. . . " while drawing in one more dot in the bottom row (figure d).* Child 3: "Yes, and I know five is one less than six."

Even when a problem is not presented visually, teachers can encourage children to recruit their spatial intelligence to find a solution. Before solving a word problem, take the time to ask children to visualize the situation. Tell them to think about the story and encourage them to create a mental picture of what is happening. Have different children explain the way that they solved the problem. As children explain their thinking, create drawings, number lines, or diagrams on the board that represent their ideas and strategies so that others can visualize the solution method. Concept Box 2.3 illustrates some of the many ways that children can think about solving the same problem, and the ways that a teacher might represent each child's strategy. When the teacher visually represents the children's thinking for everyone to see, he or she is supporting all children—both those who used the strategy and others—in using visual and spatial reasoning in problem-solving.

Concept Box 2.3   Illustrating Children's Thinking Using Visual Representations

Children are given the following story problem to solve on their own: *There were 13 blocks on the shelf. Carrie and Major used 6 of them to finish building their tower. How many blocks were left on the shelf?* The teacher then calls on individual children to explain their thinking, and she draws on the board to illustrate what they are explaining, confirming with the child that the drawing portrays their thinking.

Child's explanation	What teacher draws on board
Child 1: "I pulled out 13 chips to be blocks, then took 6 away, then counted 7 blocks left."	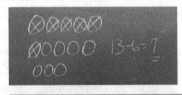
Child 2: "I started with 13 and used my fingers to count down 6, and I ended up with 7: 7 blocks on the shelf." Teacher models using her fingers, and also writes the numerals and number sentence.	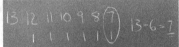

Child's explanation	What teacher draws on board
Child 3: "I started at 6 and used my fingers to count up to 13. It took 7 fingers, so that's 7 blocks." Teacher models using her fingers, and also writes the numerals and number sentence.	
Child 4: "I know that 6 is 3 + 3. I subtracted 3 from 13 to get to 10, then I subtracted 3 more, and that's 7: 7 blocks." Teacher represents the solution on a number line.	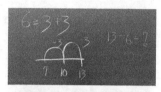
Child 5: "I know that 6 + 6 = 12. I need 1 more to get to 13, so that's 6 + 1, which is 7. So there are 7 blocks left on the shelf." Teacher represents the solution on a number line.	

Parental Input: The Untapped Resource

◆ *Parents are a child's first and most influential teachers. For the past few years, I took the parent conference as an opportunity to help parents understand their role in supporting their child's mathematics learning. I got them involved in doing the math.*

◆ *Many of my parents read to their children often, but when talking about math, they think that's teachers' responsibility. I invite them to be my partner in supporting their child's math learning by showing them the math activities we do in the classroom and how they can extend such activities at home.*

Children need to receive mathematical input not just from their teachers but also from their parents. Teachers can encourage parents to engage with children around math in ways that encourage meaningful thinking and problem solving. There are many home situations that include mathematical ideas, such as sorting laundry, setting the table, cooking, budgeting, and scheduling. Teachers can share ideas for math "conversation starters" (see Concept Box 2.4 for examples) in newsletters, on bulletin boards, during drop-off or pick-up, or at parent meetings.

Concept Box 2.4   Examples of Math Conversation Starters

Math Talk at Meal Time

◆ You are drinking from a tall, skinny glass; your child is drinking from a shorter, wider glass.
  – Say, "I wonder who has more to drink—you or me?"
  – After your child answers, say, "Why do you think so?"

◆ When the meal is over, you are putting away extra food.
  – Ask your child which container to use.
  – After your child chooses one, say, "Why do you think that one will work?"

Math Talk While Walking With Your Child

◆ "We are going downstairs, let's count **how many** steps we will need to get to the bottom."

◆ "We are going to make a turn at the **next** block. Should we turn **left or right** to get to the school?"

◆ "Have you noticed a pattern when we walk (left foot, right foot. . .)? Can you create a different walking pattern (left, right and right . . . Left, left, and right, right. . .)? How about our hands' movement when we walk?

Books are also powerful tools for supporting parents in interacting with their children about math. Most parents are already used to reading books with their children, so teachers can encourage math conversations by helping families find the math in books. This can be done through "book activity cards" that, for particular books, point out the math content, suggest questions to ask or comments to make during or after reading, and make connections between the math in the book and math in real life. For example, a book activity card for the book *A Pair of Socks* by Stuart Murphy might encourage parents to follow up by sorting laundry or finding a missing sock. It could suggest ways to have a conversation about the "rule" used for sorting or the attribute(s) used to find the missing sock. A book activity card for the book *Five Creatures* by Emily Jenkins might suggest that a family sort themselves by different rules, such as by hair length (e.g., two family members have long hair and three have short hair) or by glasses wearers (e.g., four wear glasses and one doesn't). Families can document the activity by creating pages that illustrate each sort. Math conversation starters and math book activity cards will not only foster effective mathematical input, but also help families have fun together with math.

The Bottom Line

Adult and environmental mathematical input comes in many forms. Mix's work tells us that the particular type of input can make a difference in children's learning. Further, her research suggests that this may be due to structural and visual-spatial features that help children make certain connections.

The teachers who read about the research had many ideas for ways to use this information to support learning. First, teachers can choose and arrange materials and activities that highlight these connections. Second, they can have conversations with children to make these connections more explicit. Third, they can support children's use of visual-spatial strategies to solve problems through modeling. Still, Mix points out that we may not have to look far to find particular types of input that help children, or work hard to encourage certain types of play: as she said, "many of the activities that are turning out [in research studies] to be of great benefit to young children—things like block play, making patterns, completing shape puzzles—are classic early childhood activities that kids have always loved."

Key Research Studies Discussed

Cheng, Y., and Mix, K. S. (2014). Spatial training improves children's mathematics ability. *Journal of Cognition and Development, 15*(1), 2–11.

Gentner, D. (2005). The development of relational category knowledge. *Building Object Categories in Developmental Time,* 245–275. Hove, UK: Psychology Press.

Mix, K. S., Moore, J. A., and Holcomb, E. (2011). One-to-one play promotes numerical equivalence concepts. *Journal of Cognition and Development*, 12(4), 463–480.

Mix, K. S., Sandhofer, C. M., Moore, J. A., and Russell, C. (2012). Acquisition of the cardinal word principle: The role of input. *Early Childhood Research Quarterly*, 27, 274–283.

3

The Use of Concrete Objects in Early Mathematical Learning

Jie-Qi Chen and Jeanine O'Nan Brownell, with David Uttal

The use of concrete objects, or manipulatives, to foster mathematical learning is a common practice in many early childhood classrooms. The approach is regarded as developmentally appropriate because it allows young children to learn through hands-on experiences with objects they can hold and manipulate. Though the practice is virtually universal, some studies show that young children do not make connections between their experiences with manipulatives and the mathematical concepts they are designed to teach. Why don't children make the connections? Does this mean that teachers should not use manipulatives to help children learn early math?

To explore these questions, we interviewed David Uttal, a professor of psychology and education at Northwestern University. Uttal's research covers a wide range of topics in cognitive development, including mental representation, spatial reasoning, and early symbolization. In this chapter, we focus on his work related to children's understanding of symbols and explore what this research suggests about the practice of using manipulatives.

Concept Box 3.1   What Are Manipulatives?

Manipulatives take many forms. Some are objects that were designed for specific types of mathematics learning, such as Cuisenaire Rods and Dienes Blocks. Others are materials that are commonly found in classrooms but are used for a variety of purposes, such as Unifix cubes, pattern blocks, and counting bears. Still others are household objects such as paper clips, coins, cereal, and crackers. According to Uttal, regardless of the type, what makes an object a manipulative is the fact that a teacher can use it to help children learn mathematical concepts.

The use of manipulatives is based on theories about young children's learning and development by theorists such as Friedrich Froebel, Jean Piaget, Jerome Bruner, and Maria Montessori. The theories maintain that young children are *concrete* thinkers, while mathematical concepts are *abstract*. These theories also assert that young children are active learners; they must construct their own knowledge in order to understand the world. Thus, for children to learn abstract mathematical concepts, the concepts need to be translated into objects that young children can see and touch. This helps them build mental images that support the development of their understanding of abstract ideas.

What the Research Says

Uttal's interest in the role of concrete objects in children's learning can be traced back to his time as a doctoral student at the University of Michigan. One of his mentors, Harold Stevenson, was one of the first American psychologists who studied Chinese and Japanese school achievement. In his seminar at the University of Michigan, recalled Uttal, Stevenson spoke often about the use of teaching tools and curricular methods in Chinese and Japanese classrooms. In Japanese classrooms, for example, Stevenson noted that teachers tended to use, again and again, a small manipulative set consisting of a few simple tools such as blocks and other shapes. Children would pull out the kit, apply it to different kinds of math problems, and in the process, become very familiar with it. Although the tools were not new, children would apply them to new problems. In contrast, American teachers sought variety. They might use Popsicle sticks in one lesson and marbles, Cheerios, M&Ms, checkers, poker chips, or plastic animals in another. To Uttal, Stevenson's observation was thought-provoking. Does type of manipulative matter? Do variety and novelty help? Years later, Uttal worked with Judy Deloache in her lab at the University of Illinois at Urbana-Champaign and participated in her "scale model" studies that examined the development of symbolic thinking. As he worked on these studies, he remembered his conversations with Stevenson about manipulatives and saw a connection between the two ideas.

Scale Model Task and the Dual Representation Hypothesis

Judy Deloache's studies used the "scale model" task to test whether young children can understand that one object can represent another object. Central to the task are two rooms: a normal-sized room furnished with a sofa, chairs, a table, and so on, and an exact replica of the normal-sized room that is similar in size to a dollhouse (see Figure 3.1). In the experiment, a child is first introduced to the model room. While the child watches, the experimenter hides a "Small Snoopy" dog under a cushion on the sofa in the model room. Then the experimenter explains that there is also a "Big Snoopy" who lives in a big room that looks just like the small room, and he is hiding at the exact place that Small Snoopy is hiding in the small room. The experimenter takes the child into the actual room and asks her to find "Big Snoopy," reminding her again that it is in the same place that Small Snoopy was in the small room.

Studying children from two to four years of age, the researchers found that children younger than three almost always failed to locate Big Snoopy in the actual room, finding it on average only about 20% of the time. What do these difficulties mean? Could it be that these children simply forgot where Little Snoopy was hidden in the model room? To check this, the experimenters took children back to look at the model after their search for Big Snoopy. The children readily located the Small Snoopy under the cushion on the small sofa. Their difficulty in locating Big Snoopy was not due to a problem with memory. Rather, they were not able to use Small Snoopy's location in the model to help them find Big Snoopy in the actual room.

Deloache and her colleagues explained this phenomenon with the *dual representation hypothesis*. According to this hypothesis, the reason the two year olds could not locate Big Snoopy was that they did not understand the relationship between the model and the actual room. Specifically, they did not see that the model could be viewed as a

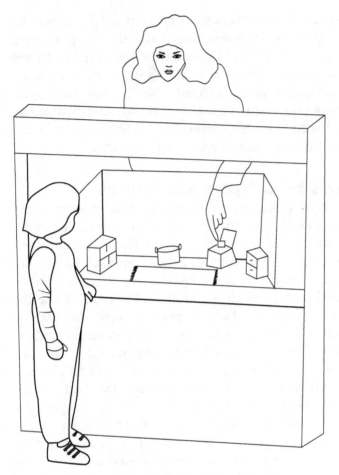

Figure 3.1 Scale model in Judy Deloache's experiment

symbol that represented the room next door. In other words, the children were incapable of representing a concrete object as both an object in and of itself and as a symbol representing something else.

To test this hypothesis, Deloache and her colleagues conducted another version of the study in which children were introduced to a "special machine" that could "shrink" large rooms (see Figure 3.2). The child watched as the experimenter hid a large troll doll in a large portable tent. Then the child left the room, and the experimenter pretended to turn on the machine. While the machine made a noise, the child was told that the room was shrinking. When they entered the room again, in place of the tent was an exact replica of the room, only smaller. This time the children were much more successful in locating the troll doll than they were in the Snoopy task. Why were they successful this time? The researchers argued that since children thought the small model and the large tent were the *same object*, they did not need to see the model as both an object and a symbol. In other words, they did not need to use dual representation to solve the problem.

Manipulatives as Symbols of Math Concepts

What does the scale model task have to do with manipulatives? When used to support the acquisition of mathematical concepts, a manipulative is like the model of the room: it is both a concrete object and a symbol that represents something else—a mathematical idea. When

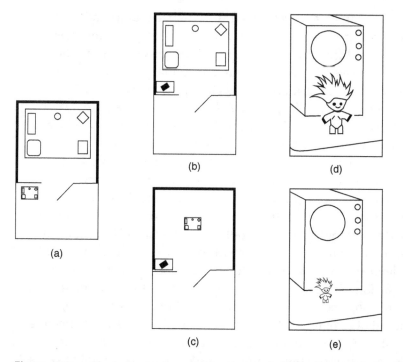

Figure 3.2a–e Physical arrangements for the symbolic and nonsymbolic tasks. For the symbolic task (a), the portable room was located in a large lab, surrounded on three sides by opaque curtains (represented by heavy lines); the model was located in an adjoining area. The nonsymbolic task began with the arrangement shown in (b); before the first shrinking event, the portable room was located in the lab, partially surrounded by curtains, just as it was for the symbolic task. The only difference was the presence of the shrinking machine, represented by the dark rectangle, sitting on a table. In the aftermath of the shrinking event, depicted in (c), the model sat in the middle of the area previously occupied by the portable room. The sketches in (d) and (e) show Terry the Troll before and after the demonstration shrinking event.

Uttal observed children's difficulty connecting the model to the actual room in the scale model task, he wondered if they might have difficulty connecting manipulatives to the math concepts they are designed to represent. As Uttal explains it, in order for manipulatives to help children learn, children must understand that the manipulatives *represent a concept in mathematics*. He and his colleagues subsequently wrote several papers exploring these ideas. In these papers, they discussed the relation between concrete and abstract learning while exploring the kind of thinking required to learn using manipulatives.

Concept Box 3.2 Do Manipulatives Work?

Many researchers have looked at whether manipulatives help children learn the mathematical concepts they are intended to teach. It is difficult to draw a general conclusion about whether they work overall, because there are so many different contexts and ways to use manipulatives. Recently, researcher Kira Carbonneau and her colleagues (2013) conducted a meta-analysis on the topic, examining 55 studies that compared outcomes when students were taught with or without manipulatives.

Some of these studies found that children performed better with manipulatives, whereas others showed that they performed about the same as children who did not use manipulatives. A few found that children actually performed worse with manipulatives than without them. Overall, Carbonneau and her colleagues found that manipulatives seemed to help students to a small to moderate degree, but that the effects were influenced by several factors, including math content, amount of accompanying instruction, and age of the students. With regard to age, they found that the instruction with manipulatives was least effective for children between the ages of three and six years compared to older age groups (seven- to eleven-year-olds, and twelve years and older).

The researchers also called into question the idea of using manipulatives in spontaneous, self-directed play. Teachers frequently use manipulatives as a self-guided tool for mathematical learning, but it is not clear that children understand the relation between the manipulatives and the math concept they represent during this kind of play. After all, to quote the math educator Deborah Ball, "understanding does not travel through the fingertips and up the arm . . . Mathematical ideas really do not reside in cardboard and plastic materials" (1992; p. 47). Uttal and his colleagues argued that it is unlikely that young children directly perceive the relation between manipulatives and abstract mathematical concepts and symbols. Rather, their comprehension of these relations needs to be guided by teachers' instruction.

Factors That Affect Children's Ability to Use the Model as a Symbol

Deloache, Uttal, and their colleagues conducted further experiments using the scale model task to find out whether any particular factors affect children's ability to achieve dual representation—that is, to be able to view the model as a symbol of the larger room. In one experiment, children were allowed to play with the room model for five to ten minutes before they were asked to locate Big Snoopy in the actual room. These children were less successful in locating Big Snoopy than children who did not play with the model. Other children saw only a picture of the room model, and still others saw the model but were not able to touch it because it was placed behind glass. Both of these conditions improved children's performance on the task.

Why would more time with the model in the above experiment matter, and why would contact with an actual model versus a picture, or viewing a model behind glass matter? The researchers explained that playing with the actual model beforehand led children to focus on it as an interesting toy. They consequently had more difficulty thinking of the model as a representation of the room. When the model was shown as a picture or was not accessible to play with, they were more likely to be able to view it as a symbol of the actual room.

In another variation of the study, researchers modified the instructions children were given about the relationship between the room model and the actual room. In one condition, the experimenters proceeded as they did in the usual version of the study, calling children's attention to the detailed similarities between the model and actual room. For example, they brought the small couch into the actual room and said, "Look—this is Big Snoopy's big couch, and this is Little

Snoopy's little couch. They're just the same." In the other condition, they omitted this part of the instructions. Children were less successful at finding Big Snoopy when the similarities between the rooms were not made explicit; these children succeeded at chance level (i.e., at the same rate as if they were just guessing). Thus, without instructions, children were not able to see how the model room related to the room next door. They needed an adult to show and tell them that the model represented the actual room.

Teacher Responses

◆ *I was once told to let children "play" with the math materials for a while first before using them for math. My instinct, however, was to not to let them play with the materials until after they had learned the "math use" for them. So, the finding that children who were allowed to play with the model room for five to ten minutes beforehand were less successful in finding Snoopy resonates with me.*

◆ *I had a student who had difficulty creating a pattern with colorful Legos at one point in the year. Based on the reading, I wondered if, similar to the students who played with the scale model room before they were asked to locate Big Snoopy in the actual room, he had difficulty with the creation of the pattern not because he did not understand the mathematical concept of a pattern, but because those Legos were seen as a building toy first and foremost in his play. Given that possibility, it may have made it too difficult to see the Legos as only a symbol for pieces of a pattern.*

Concept Box 3.3   Concrete and Abstract Thinking in Mathematics

As described in Box 3.1, many theorists have argued that children learn through concrete experiences. To learn mathematics, though, children must grasp ideas that are abstract. Even basic math concepts, such as number, are abstract. For example, when a teacher is helping young children learn the concept of four, she may place four paper cups on the table. Cups are concrete objects that children know can be used to drink milk, juice, or water. However, in this situation, the function of the cups, as well as the particular shape, size, or color, does not matter. What matters is the quantity that the objects *represent*: the cardinal number four (for a detailed explanation of cardinal numbers, see Chapter 1, Concept Box 1.2). Four is an abstract concept: the "fourness" of the four cups has no direct relation to the objects—they could be cups or spoons, red or blue.

Uttal asserts that mathematics at its core is an abstract system. Learning the meaning of the word "four" (and eventually the symbol "4") allows children to reason about numerical relations independent of any physical representation of the concepts. For example, as he explains in one paper, one can figure out the solution to the question, "What is one more than four?" without thinking, "four of what?" or "one more of what?" So, to be able to engage in mathematical thinking, he concludes, children must acquire a system that is "distinctly *not concrete.*" Uttal ponders how the transition from concrete thinking (focusing on the actual cups) to abstract thinking (considering the quantity four, and figuring out what one more than four is) occurs and whether this is always the direction of learning.

Teacher Responses

◆ *I recognize characteristics of both concrete and abstract thinking present in children's play and learning. But I have difficulty conceiving of how children might learn certain concepts, such as basic cardinality of number, without dependence on concrete objects. I once used dot cards that represent numbers 1 to 10 to help children develop a mental visual representation of the number. In this example, children don't physically manipulate any objects and yet they are doing very well with the task. Is this an example of mathematical thinking that may not necessarily progress from concrete to abstract? Where does pictorial representation or visual image fit into this developmental trajectory?*

Perceptually Rich Manipulatives in Early Math Learning

In recent years, Uttal and his colleagues investigated the idea of whether making manipulatives more attractive affects children's gains from them. They looked specifically at a manipulative system called Digi-Blocks. The system includes blocks representing ones, tens, hundreds, and so on, where ten "one" blocks fit inside a "ten" block, and ten "tens" fit inside a "one hundred" block. Digi-Blocks are designed to help children understand place value, including arithmetic problems that require "carryover" or "borrowing." For example, when solving 31–22, a child must figure out how to take away the 2 from 1 in the units column. With the Digi-Blocks, they can take a "ten" block, open it to reveal ten "one" blocks, and then use the eleven "ones" to subtract two (see Figure 3.3).

The researchers had previously found that children who were instructed with Digi-Blocks learned to solve "carryover" problems using the blocks, although they could not immediately transfer this knowledge to an equivalent problem in written form. In this experiment, the researchers explored whether making the manipulatives perceptually attractive affected children's ability to use the blocks to solve problems. Two groups of children who had just finished the first grade participated in the experiment. One group was assigned to use the standard manipulatives while the other used a distinctive set that was decorated with different colors and unique designs such as swirls and polka dots. Children were asked to use the manipulatives to solve two-digit subtraction problems that required the "borrowing" or "carryover" method for solution.

The results showed that, although not statistically significant, the standard manipulatives group performed better than the distinctive manipulatives group. Children in the distinctive group were more likely to play with the blocks (e.g., build towers) than use them to solve the problems. Furthermore, children in the distinctive group were less likely to use the proper procedures and therefore more likely to make errors in calculation than those in the standard group. Based on the results, Uttal and colleagues concluded that "visually distinctive, compared with standard, manipulatives tended to detract from mathematics instruction."

Teacher Responses

◆ *The finding about the difference between distinctive and standard Digi-Blocks was particularly poignant to me. It reminds me of how, especially with young children, sorting materials with multiple attributes can be difficult. Students are asked to ignore extremely salient attributes such as color in order to sort by shape, size, or some other attribute entirely.*

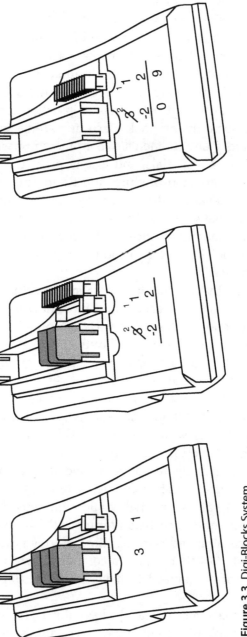

Figure 3.3 Digi-Blocks System

Challenges in Studying the Efficacy of Teaching Early Math With Manipulatives

Although he writes extensively about mathematical learning with manipulatives, Uttal is keenly aware of the limitations of the scale model studies and other developmental psychology research he conducted in terms of having clear implications for classroom practice. The scale model studies, for example, were not designed to directly examine the relationship between manipulatives and mathematical learning. The experiments took place in well-designed, highly controlled laboratory environments, where the emphasis is on rigorous control of subjects, materials, and testing procedures. In classrooms, however, variations in procedures are the norm, and materials are adapted to be relevant to the context. In fact, the more Uttal explored the relationship between manipulatives and math learning, the more he realized both the significance and the complexity of the issue. In his words, "The problem is too rich and too important to be based on just laboratory studies."

Recognizing the constraints of the laboratory study, Uttal attempted to work with classroom teachers to explore how manipulatives affect math learning and teaching. He was confronted with a number of challenges. For example, to study the effectiveness of manipulatives in math learning, he would need to compare two groups of classrooms, where one group would use manipulatives for math learning and the other would not. However, for most teachers, particularly those working in early childhood classrooms, the idea of giving up the use of manipulatives would be unthinkable. Further, to gain a deep understanding of the impact of manipulatives on math learning, he would need to investigate the issue under different circumstances, varying type of manipulative, frequency of use, and details of associated instruction—all factors that would require teacher collaboration. However, while many teachers are interested in exploring different methods of teaching and learning, they are often cautious about participating in studies that require a commitment of instructional time but that are not guaranteed to have a positive impact on students' performance.

Uttal said that over the years he has gained a more nuanced understanding of the role of manipulatives in children's learning by observing classrooms and conversing with teachers. For example, he recalled, a kindergarten teacher once told him about children playing with pretend spaghetti using either yarn or real-looking plastic spaghetti. The teacher noticed that if children first used the plastic spaghetti, they had difficulty later seeing the yarn as spaghetti. If they did not use the plastic spaghetti first, they were much more able to view the yarn as representing spaghetti. To Uttal, this aligned with his viewpoint that the type of manipulative, specifically how realistic it is, matters. The teacher's observations suggested that representing objects with manipulatives that are too realistic may prevent children from seeing that those objects can be represented in a different way.

Teacher Responses

- *This resonated with my experiences in huge ways. It reminded me of a play kitchen I used to have in my classroom. The kitchen had a lot of realistic materials made out of plastic or wood, such as stove, refrigerator, plates, fruit, and vegetables. It sat underneath a loft in the room and remained there for a year, and even when we used thematic units to change our loft into a rainforest or a boat, the students still routinely played pretend restaurant or house underneath the loft. The following year, I removed the kitchen, and found that children began to engage in other thematic play. To me, this feels similar to the yarn and spaghetti, in that when the spaghetti was introduced first, it's much harder for children to engage in the symbolic substitution of other materials.*

- *I have similarly observed that when you present manipulatives with a very specific purpose, students have difficulty seeing how they can use those in different ways. When I worked with preschoolers, I saw children being more open to using things in different ways and creating "tools" that they could use to solve problems. When I started teaching first grade, I saw the difference since children were not so willing to try things on their own and always looked for my guidance to tell them how to use things specifically. Now that I teach third grade I have to guide my students to find different uses for different things, and it is almost like going backwards in the process of teaching them that manipulatives can be used in different ways to solve different problems.*

- *This makes me think about playgrounds and structures for playing: those that are less realistic or defined leave more room for creative interpretation. An example is building a house or castle out of*

blocks versus playing with a manufactured play house or castle.
That block castle is destructible and can be something new the next
time you play or can be tweaked depending upon who moves in or
moves out of the castle.

Uttal believes that these types of conversations can guide research.
So, he suggests, rather than designing a teaching method in a laboratory setting and then asking whether it would work in a classroom,
researchers could first consider issues that arise in classrooms and then
design corresponding experiments. To gain a deep understanding of
mathematics learning in the classroom, Uttal believes that researchers need to engage in "a serious partnership with educators, teachers,
principals, and parents."

Conclusion

Uttal and the other researchers cited here do not dispute the fact that
manipulatives serve a critical function in early mathematics education.
Concrete objects can help children learn math concepts that might
otherwise remain abstract and inaccessible. However, these researchers point out that children may not understand that a manipulative is
intended to also represent something else—in other words, that it is a
symbol. Thus, when using concrete objects in early mathematics education, they argue that teachers should consider whether children are
able or likely to engage in dual representation—that is, understanding
that manipulatives are both objects in and of themselves and symbols
that represent mathematical concepts.

Teachers Respond to the Research

Teachers found the topic very interesting, as manipulatives are often
perceived as a requirement for math learning in early childhood classrooms. They understood the connections that Uttal made between the
manipulatives and the scale models, in that both are concrete objects
but also symbolic representations of something else. They agreed that
adults must play a role in helping the child make a connection between
the object and the symbol. In one teacher's words, "accompanying
instruction in the child's use of manipulatives for math instruction is
a necessity."

Teachers were aware that there is a lack of empirical studies that directly address the effects of manipulatives on early math learning. They tended to agree that it would be hard for teachers to take the chance to participate in a research study when a child's learning would be at stake with no guarantee of improvement over current practices. However, many teachers said that they would be interested in working with a researcher to explore ways that manipulatives can be used appropriately to facilitate young children's mathematical learning. Teachers' reactions to the research are grouped into five topics below.

Manipulatives and the Related Mathematical Concepts

In the seminar, the teachers examined a range of manipulatives commonly used in the classroom for math activities, such as counting bears, interlocking cubes, base-10 blocks, pattern blocks, Rekenreks (arithmetic racks, see Figure 3.4), unit blocks, and so on. They were asked to discuss the ways in which they use these materials with children. Teachers soon realized that some manipulatives, such as base-10 blocks and Rekenreks, are geared to specific mathematical concepts, whereas other materials lend themselves to multiple ideas. For example, interlocking cubes can be used for both counting and measurement, and pattern blocks for both shapes and fractions. **When should teachers use manipulatives that are designed for specific math concepts versus those that can be used to teach multiple ideas?**

David Uttal's Response

This is a very interesting and important question. I think in addressing it, we should keep in mind how students may think about different kinds of manipulatives. The introduction of each new manipulative requires that students think about and become familiar with another physical object. Although the intended use of the manipulative may be clear to the teacher, students have to construct in their own minds

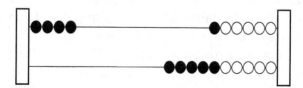

Figure 3.4 Rekenrek

how the intended referent relates to the intended mathematics concept. With frequent changes of manipulatives, this may be harder to do.

Let me answer the question more directly: My reading of the literature suggests that *fewer is better*; that the use of a few relevant manipulatives is likely to be more successful than frequently changing the manipulatives *when introducing new mathematics concepts*. In choosing manipulatives, teachers can think about which manipulatives offer the broadest "coverage" for a variety of mathematics concepts.

Manipulatives and Type of Mathematical Tasks

Several teachers commented that, in their experience, the use of manipulatives for certain basic early math concepts such as counting with one-to-one correspondence, cardinality, and numeral representations is hugely successful. One teacher said she doesn't dare teach or show any a numeral without a manipulative to go with it. On the other hand, they said that when manipulatives are used to represent stories, scenarios, and more complex problems, they seem to get in the way of the concept: the manipulatives can become an extra step in the process and cause confusion. One teacher tested this hypothesis. When conducting the end-of-year assessment of story problems, she gave some of her kindergarteners a dry erase board. Children could draw a picture or use fingers or mental arithmetic to solve the problem. These children seemed to do better than those who had manipulatives. The teacher found that children who used manipulatives were more likely to forget the point of the problem and just start counting randomly. For story problems, teachers found it helpful to use pictures, rather than manipulatives, to represent the objects in the story, or to have children act it out. **Does the usefulness of manipulatives vary by mathematical tasks?**

David Uttal's Response

I think the answer is likely "yes," although I am not aware of systematic research on this question. The teachers' observation that manipulatives are likely to be most important or effective when teaching basic concepts, such as cardinality, is an intriguing idea. Likewise, I also agree that manipulatives may be more distracting, requiring an "extra step," in solving more complex problems. These questions also point again to the need for more *systematic research on when and why* manipulatives are helpful, as opposed to *"whether" they are helpful*.

Manipulatives and Dual Representation

Teachers wondered about the relation between the different types of manipulatives mentioned in Concept Box 3.1 and the level of dual representation required to understand the relationship between the manipulative and the math concept. If we use daily objects such as paper clips, crackers, and coins as math manipulatives, dual representation seems necessary. For children, paper clips are for holding paper and crackers are for eating. To understand their connection to a math concept, children must go beyond the defined and familiar functions of these household objects. Other manipulatives such as base-10 blocks or Digi-Blocks directly represent the math concept—place value in this case. They are standardized tools designed to help children learn procedures. Children do not seem to need dual representation when using this type of manipulatives. **Must children understand that "manipulatives represent a concept in mathematics" in order for manipulatives to help them learn?**

David Uttal's Response

My thinking about this issue has evolved considerably since publishing our original paper on the issue of dual representation and manipulative use in the late 1990s. At that time, my colleagues and I claimed that children had to obtain dual-representation in order to effectively use all manipulatives. We asserted that the children had to see the manipulatives as symbolic representations that related to the mathematics concepts that they were learning.

I now believe that much of the advantage of manipulatives may stem in part from the fact that they do *not* necessarily need to be seen as representations of mathematical concepts—that the concepts may in fact emerge in part through physical interactions with the manipulatives. For example, children's mathematical concept of sets can be developed through by playing with toys such as stacking cups. This change of thought came about as the result of a series of studies by other researchers (e.g., Martin & Schwartz, 2005; Son, Smith, & Goldstone, 2008) who challenged the idea that early mathematical thinking needs to be necessarily symbolic in nature.

Type and Variety of Manipulatives

Teachers were intrigued to learn that a small set of tools is used over and over in Japanese classrooms to teach math concepts. They saw the potential value of such practice because children don't have to clear the hurdle of dual representation every time they learn a new concept. On the other hand, they wondered whether variety in manipulatives might help children generalize an understanding beyond a specific kind of manipulative and emphasize the abstract nature of math concepts. For example, it may help a child understand the "fourness" of four described in Concept Box 3.3 if they see four represented with many different kinds of manipulatives, such as interlocking cubes, dice, and round counters of many colors. **Is one of these approaches (less versus more variety in manipulatives) more beneficial for children's learning? Is there a general principle that might guide teachers in deciding how much variety to use in their math manipulatives?**

David Uttal's Response

Perhaps one general principle would be this: Choose the manipulative that allows for the most mathematical teaching and learning with the least emphasis on the properties of the objects themselves. In some cases, highly specialized manipulatives that represent particular concepts (e.g., base-10 blocks for place value) may be particularly helpful, but this potential benefit needs to be weighed against the potential challenges that arise from introducing a new manipulative. Sometimes the simplest manipulative can be used to illustrate or facilitate a large number of concepts.

Factors That Influence Children's Capacity for Dual Representation

Teachers recognized the role that dual representation plays in using manipulatives for early math learning. They hypothesized that multiple factors could influence children's ability to engage in dual representation, including age or maturation, familiarity with the materials, language development, theory of mind, and type of manipulatives. Related to age in particular, teachers noticed in Concept Box 3.2 the finding that instruction with manipulatives was least effective for children between the ages of three and six years compared to older age groups (seven to eleven year olds and twelve years and older). They wondered how much this result relates to the development of children's dual representation. **When are children capable of dual representation? What factors are related to this capability? Is it simply a matter of age and maturation?**

David Uttal's Response

I'm afraid I'll have to give an "academic" answer to this question. I don't think of dual-representation as a single concept that is acquired at a particular age. Rather, children acquire dual representation at different ages, depending on the concepts and symbols that are being developed. For example, in some sense, language requires dual-representation; children need to focus on what the sounds represent, rather than just on the sound themselves. This understanding is reached at a very young age. In contrast, dual representation may be obtained at a much later age for less familiar concepts (including mathematics). So we cannot say simply that children acquire dual-representation at a particular age.

Teachers' Ideas for Classroom Practice

In response to issues related to the use of concrete objects in early mathematics education, teachers offered many thoughtful observations as well as useful strategies to promote children's math learning and understanding with manipulatives. Below, we present teachers' ideas within four themes: introducing new manipulatives to children, respecting children's developmental needs, selecting manipulatives, and the role of teachers in helping children learn from manipulatives.

Introducing New Manipulatives Thoughtfully

◆ *We usually start with an **open exploration** of the tool and then **students share** ways they can use that tool. Then I will **model** using the tool, and then students will use it that way and sometimes we will do a fishbowl where we watch students use the tool and **comment on their actions**.*

◆ *I teach second grade. If it is a new manipulative, I always let students kind of **explore** it first. Then I come back and say, "OK, what did your group do with that? How did you explore it? What did you notice?" and so on, and then I kind of guide that into, "OK, this is a **tool** we're going to be using to learn about math."*

◆ *I think teachers' **modeling and conversations** with their students are critical for understanding. Adults should not just assume children "get it" because they are told that one thing is now represented by something else.*

◆ *As new manipulatives are added throughout the year, we add them to a **chart**, so children can remember what we have used and how we used it. They love to see that a manipulative can be used to support multiple math concepts. I also have had students **journal** (using pictures or words) about how they used a particular manipulative. This helps students make a stronger connection between the concrete and abstract. If they can explain WHAT they are doing with the manipulatives and WHY (what are they trying to represent), then they are getting a deeper understanding. This also aids them in seeing manipulatives as representations of certain objects/concepts.*

What teachers described here reveals three key practices to use when introducing new manipulatives to young children. The first is providing students with time to explore the properties of the materials so that they can discover their mathematical qualities. Different materials might require different amounts of time. For example, time for exploring materials such as counting discs should be minimal because there is not a lot to discover about them. On the other hand, more complex manipulatives such as unit blocks or geometric solids inherently present many facets of mathematical concepts. Greater experience with such materials could yield more understanding of their mathematical functioning. Teachers also mentioned asking children to talk about their experience exploring the new manipulatives. This is beneficial for at least two reasons. First, it can give teachers insight into the features that children notice about the manipulatives—whether they are mathematical or not. Second, if children do identify mathematical qualities of the manipulatives, teachers can build on these observations during instruction.

A second practice for introducing manipulatives is intentionally modeling how to use them and talking about how one's actions in using them relate to the math concept. The importance of teachers' demonstrating and explaining how to use manipulatives is often overlooked in classroom practice. For example, many teachers use a Rekenrek (a counting frame with rows of beads that slide back and forth to keep track of amounts; see Figure 3.4) to help children learn about composing and decomposing numbers. Few, however, spend time showing and explaining to children why there are two bars on the Rekenrek and why there are two colors of beads on each bar. Such explanation primes children to use it for mathematical learning. Using the term "tool" instead of "toy" to describe manipulatives is another way to emphasize their use for solving math problems. Explicit statements about how the material represents the mathematical procedure or concept help direct children's attention to relevant features of materials.

Introducing new manipulatives should not be a one-time exercise. Rather, it should be done over several lessons in which children explore the relationship between the hands-on experience of using the tools and the minds-on exercise of constructing understanding. Documentation, the third practice brought up by the teachers, helps describe this process and provides opportunities for discussion, which often generates discovery and further learning. Having children create journal entries and keep a chart of manipulatives they have used are excellent suggestions. Drawing, graphing, and writing about how the physical objects connect with the mental processes activate their own and others' thinking, reveal potential misconceptions to the teacher, and help them see that certain manipulatives can represent a range of concepts.

Respect Children's Developmental Needs

◆ *Don't push the abstract too soon. I agree that mathematical thinking may not necessarily progress from concrete to abstract— that mathematical thinking itself is really just abstract. But I still think children's development progresses from concrete to abstract. When we push children to do more **abstract mathematical thinking too soon**, it has an **adverse effect. Children end up getting further behind when we skip steps.***

◆ *I feel many teachers try to introduce the symbolic representation too quickly, without letting children **explore the concept concretely for an extended period of time**. I think children get better at making the connection between manipulatives and concepts when you ask them to explain their thinking, as well as modeling your own thinking with the manipulatives.*

◆   *I think the **younger the learner, the more time must be devoted
    to concrete learning**. In the example presented in Concept
    Box 3.3, a child must be able to picture some sort of representation
    in their head: four dots, four cars, four cups, to truly understand
    "fourness." If not, they may have just memorized the symbol 4 and
    its name. As another example, when developing spatial awareness,
    I find that children have a better understanding and greater success
    in identifying shapes and composing/decomposing shapes when
    they have had time to concretely touch and explore the shapes.
    Most of the time young learners (and even older students) need to
    experience first-hand how shapes can slide, flip, and turn to create
    other shapes/configurations.*

These teacher comments point to the need for developmentally—
appropriate practice in early math teaching and learning. Most early
childhood teachers understand the importance of teaching math
to young children. However, if practices are not developmentally
appropriate, early math instruction could backfire. One teacher
quoted above said it well: "Children end up getting further behind
when we skip steps." A critical first step in early math learning is providing ample time for children to explore the materials, get familiar
with their distinctive features, share the experience of using them,
and be guided to make sense of their connection to math concepts.
For the developing child, getting to know materials, including math
manipulatives, requires time to see, touch, play, and test. Encouraging young children to explore is not a waste of time. It builds their
confidence as well as their understanding that the material can be
a tool for mathematical problem solving. Remember, however, the
scale model experiment in which giving children 5–10 minutes to
play with the manipulative actually resulted in poorer performance.
The key difference is how the time exploring the manipulatives is
spent: unguided play focusing on the amusing appearance of the
object versus assisted exploration focusing on the various mathematical features of the object.

The time spent exploring manipulatives is not void of symbolic or
abstract thinking. Adults need to be cognizant that at any moment of
child development, concrete, pictorial, and abstract thinking co-exist.
Thinking moves between concrete, pictorial, and abstract constantly.
As such, the more connections among the three forms of thinking we

reinforce, the more we help young children build strong and sophisticated reasoning. The goal of early math education is not simply to move young children to abstract thinking. Rather, it is to help children make sense of the relationship between concrete materials and the abstract concepts they represent.

Select Manipulatives With Care

- ◆ *Choosing manipulatives is always hard. A lot of times they don't come with our curriculum, so we're making the decisions on what we should introduce on our own. You really need to be* **mindful in choosing the materials**. *You don't want to detract from the concept.*

- ◆ *There are so many cutesy things out there. I would rather* **use a plain counter** *or a bottle cap than put a smiley face on it and think the kids are going to like it more. I don't like calling things that I'm using as a tool "cute." I think it diminishes what we're doing with young children to call it cute. And I don't think kids like them less or more just because it's got a smiley face on it, or it's cute, or it's colorful.*

- ◆ *In my experience, depending on the* **purpose of the activity**, *the things that are* **standardized mathematical tools,** *such as base-10 blocks, seem to get better* **procedural results** *than the things that are very open and playful in nature.*

- ◆ *You* **don't have to have all those store-bought manipulatives**. *You can go out and get some buttons, bottle caps, or used keys. Those things help get the concept across too.*

For manipulatives to promote mathematical learning and understanding, they must be chosen and used carefully. A good manipulative should facilitate, rather than hinder, children's perception of the relationship between the material and the math concept that the teacher intends to teach. Specifically, attractive or interesting manipulatives may sometimes be counterproductive if they draw children's attention to features such as colors and decorations that are perceptually appealing but have little to do with the mathematical concept. Likewise, manipulatives that resemble everyday objects, such as food or toys, could also distract children from seeing the symbolic meaning of the materials because of their prior experience with these objects. The example of the Japanese classroom practice described at the beginning of the chapter is a reminder of the potential benefit of using a simple and limited set of manipulatives consistently.

For a manipulative to be effective, it also needs to be used over a long period of time. Research indicates that the benefit of manipulatives depends on how long children are exposed to them. Evelyn Sowell (1989), for example, conducted a meta-analysis of 60 studies involving students from kindergarten to college and found that exposure to the same manipulative for a school year or more led to more learning than instruction with manipulatives over a shorter period of time and to instruction without manipulatives. Another study by Taylor Martin (2009) shows that using the same or similar manipulatives to repeatedly solve problems leads to a deeper understanding of the relation between the physical material and the abstract concept.

Shown in Concept Box 3.1, manipulatives take many forms. The effectiveness of any particular manipulative depends largely on the purpose of the activity. As teachers point out, if a particular procedure or concept such as place-value or the base-10 number system is the goal, manipulatives such as Digi-blocks, Cuisenaire rods, or base-10 blocks are appropriate. If cardinality (e.g., the concept of "fourness," described in Concept Box 3.3) is the goal, the teacher might want to start with one kind of material and gradually introduce others to help children understand the abstract nature of the concept. A rule of thumb is that the greater the alignment between the manipulative and the concept it represents, the more likely it is that children will be able to understand the relation between the two. This is illustrated in a study by Siegler and Ramani (2009) about how playing with number board games influences preschool children's learning of magnitude of number (how "big" a number is in comparison to another). The researchers found that playing on a game board in which the numbers 1 to 10 were arranged in a line led to better understanding of magnitude than playing a game board with the numbers arranged in a circle. The researchers believe that the linear game board works better because it is a more transparent reflection of increasing numerical magnitude.

Actively Guide the Use of Manipulatives

◆ *A child's natural response to an object is to pretend it's something else. If I give children manipulatives, they pretend they are spaceships, they build towers, they act out stories with them. But when I specify "their use" for counting, they use them to count. I have a ton of math games/activities meant for two to three players. If I put the box out without instructions, the goal of the game is never achieved—even ones that are seemingly self-explanatory, for example, a number foam cards with the corresponding number of holes. Children are supposed to count out pegs to put in the holes, and then they can see the amount of pegs that matches the number. If I just put that out, I see all kinds of imaginary play going on and never the practice of counting and representing numbers.*

◆ *Making **comments** about how children are using manipulatives helps them see what the manipulatives stand for and what concept they are demonstrating. We need to remember to **continue being explicit** with the use of manipulatives—even more so with the earliest learners.*

◆ *Sometimes I **feel hesitant to teach using manipulatives** because I feel my students will have more confusion. I now realize that the times I don't use them, it is often because **I am not familiar with them** myself; therefore I feel confused on how to introduce my students to the manipulatives.*

◆ ***Teachers don't get any training on how to use manipulatives.** If I don't know how to use them properly, I'd rather not confuse the students. I didn't grow up using counters or any of those things. I didn't know Unifix cubes could be used for measuring. It's like I don't know what to do with them. They take up space in my classroom. I find other ways to teach, and I feel like I get the concepts across. Now reading all of this and having a discussion makes me think about how I can try using different kinds of manipulatives.*

Manipulatives are tools. Teachers play a vital role in using them effectively to support children's mathematical learning. Consider the scale model experiment: the relation between the model and the real room is completely transparent for adults, but not for young children. Similarly, even with carefully designed manipulatives, children may not recognize the relationship between a concrete object and an abstract concept. As was shown in one of the scale model studies, adult guidance can help children to make this connection. Indeed, in their meta-analysis described in Concept Box 3.2, Carbonneau and colleagues (2013) found that the use of manipulatives coupled with high levels of instructional guidance contributed more to student learning than low levels of guidance did.

Instructional guidance can be both verbal and non-verbal. The research work described in Chapter 1 documents the power of mathematical language for children's learning. A teacher's math verbalizations help articulate the goal of activities, surface the opaque relation between manipulatives and the mathematical concepts they are designed to teach, and guide children toward mathematical understanding and problem solving. The research in Chapter 4 describes the effect of gestures on children's mathematical learning. More specifically, gestures are believed to play an important role in drawing children's attention to the connection between two representations. For example, a teacher who uses her hands to circle a group of four cups while saying, "Here are four cups," is using gesture to help children understand the connection between concrete (physical) and symbolic (linguistic) representations of cardinality.

Although manipulatives are seen in almost all American early childhood classrooms, few pre-service or in-service teacher training programs focus specifically on the topic of how to use manipulatives effectively in early math education. As it is unreasonable to expect children themselves to make the connection between manipulatives and their intended math concepts, it is equally unfair to expect teachers to use the manipulatives effectively in their teaching if they never used them when they learned math and were never taught how to use them in teaching. The primary reason for the limited practical guidance in using manipulatives is our limited understanding of the topic. Discussed earlier in the chapter, few empirical research studies have been conducted in the area. We have little empirical evidence, for example, that indicates how soon and how often children should use manipulatives for math learning. One goal of this chapter is to raise awareness that research on the use of concrete objects in early mathematics learning deserves greater attention.

The Bottom Line

In the field of early childhood education, the role of manipulatives in math learning is rarely questioned. We now know, however, that manipulatives can either facilitate or hinder young children's appreciation of the relationships between concrete objects and their intended referents or mathematical concepts. Used appropriately, manipulatives can support the development of abstract mathematical concepts by linking them to concrete physical actions and mental images. Used inappropriately, manipulatives can distract children from math learning by turning their attention to irrelevant features.

Teachers play a critical role in helping children learn from manipulatives: they must guide students toward math discoveries from the manipulatives. This guidance can be both verbal and non-verbal. In either case, the purpose is to help children make the connection between manipulatives and the math concepts that teachers intend to teach. Research on the role of manipulatives in early math learning is still in its infancy. It is imperative that teachers and developmental psychologists work together to study this relatively unexplored territory.

Key Research Studies Discussed

Ball, D. (1992). Magical hopes: Manipulatives and the reform of math education. *American Educators, 6*, 1418.

Carbonneau, K. J., Marley, S. C., and Selig, J. P. (2013). A meta-analysis of the efficacy of teaching mathematics with concrete manipulatives. *Journal of Educational Psychology, 105*(2), 380–400.

DeLoache, J. S., Miller, K. F., and Rosengren, K. S. (1997). The credible shrinking room: Very young children's performance with symbolic and nonsymbolic relations. *Psychological Science, 8*(4), 308–313.

Deloache, J. S., Uttal, D. H., and Pierroutsakos, S. L. (1998). The development of early symbolization: Educational implications. *Learning and Instruction, 8*(4), 325–339.

Martin, T. (2009). A theory of physically distributed learning: How external environments and internal states interact in mathematical learning. *Child Development Perspectives, 3*, 140–144.

Martin, T., and Schwartz, D. L. (2005). Physically distributed learning: Adapting and reinterpreting physical environments in the development of fraction concepts. *Cognitive Science, 29*(4), 587–625.

Siegler, S. R., and Ramani, G. B. (2009). Playing linear number board games-but not circular ones-improves low-income preschoolers' numerical understanding. *Journal of Educational Psychology, 10*(3), 545–560.

Son, J. Y., Smith, L. B., and Goldstone, R. L. (2008). Simplicity and generalization: Short-cutting abstraction in children's object categorizations. *Cognition, 108*(3), 626–638.

Sowell, E. J. (1989). Effects of manipulative materials in mathematics instruction. *Journal of Research in Mathematics Education, 20*, 498–505.

Uttal, D. H., Amaya, M., del Rosario Maita, M., Hand, L. L., Cohen, C. A., O'Doherty, K., and DeLoache, J. S. (2013). It works both ways: Transfer difficulties between manipulatives and written subtraction solutions. *Child Development Research.* Retrieved from groups.psych.northwestern.edu/uttal/documents/Uttaletal2013.pdf

Uttal, D. H., Scudder, K. V., and DeLoache, J. S. (1997). Manipulatives as symbols: A new perspective on the use of concrete objects to teach mathematics. *Journal of Applied Developmental Psychology, 18*, 37–54.

The Role of Gesture in Teaching and Learning Math

*Mary Hynes-Berry and Jennifer S. McCray,
with Susan Goldin-Meadow*

Whether we are chatting with friends, giving directions about how to get somewhere, or explaining how we solved a problem, our hands are often moving. Interestingly, while we may be conscious of the words we are using, we are usually not even aware that we are gesturing, much less that we are sending important additional information with our gestures. Although gestures are spontaneous and vary from individual to individual, they often reinforce or clarify the information found in speech, adding new information as well as nuance. For this chapter, we interview Susan Goldin-Meadow, a professor of psychology at the University of Chicago, who studies non-verbal communication with specific emphasis on gestures. Goldin-Meadow's research provides strong evidence that gestures play an important role not only in reflecting and communicating our thoughts, but also in changing those thoughts. Although her work on the topic is far-reaching, in this chapter, we will be looking specifically at the role of gesture in the development of young children's understanding of mathematics.

Background

Goldin-Meadow spent her college junior year in Geneva, Switzerland, where she had the amazing good fortune to take classes with Jean Piaget, the founding father of research in cognitive development. Piaget insisted that genuine understanding results from the learner actively constructing meaning, rather than passively accepting direct instruction from a teacher. Goldin-Meadow's interest in how children represent meaning through gesture is grounded in this theory.

Goldin-Meadow's doctoral dissertation grew out of a deep interest in where language comes from. She looked at deaf children born to hearing parents who did not expose them to sign language. While their hearing losses meant they didn't acquire spoken language, nevertheless they did construct a manual language, called "homesign," using gesture. She was interested in the ways that these homesign languages are related to, but also quite different from, the gestures that hearing people produce when they talk. That study set off an inquiry into the relationship between language, gesture, and cognition that she has continued to investigate ever since.

What the Research Says

"Mismatches" Between Speech and Gesture in Conservation Tasks

One of Goldin-Meadow's early findings regarding the role of gesture in learning emerged when she was reexamining tasks made famous by Piaget—specifically tasks that assess children's understanding of *conservation* (see Concept Box 4.1). To better understand Goldin-Meadow's research, let's first consider Piaget's classic conservation of liquid task (see Figure 4.1). In this task, an interviewer first pours the same amount of liquid into two identical short, wide glasses and has the child verbally confirm that the amounts in both glasses are equal. The child then watches as the interviewer pours the liquid from one of the glasses into a taller, narrower glass. Now looking at two glasses, one short and wide, and the other tall and narrow, the child is asked: "Is there the *same* or a *different* amount of liquid in both glasses?"

Concept Box 4.1   Piaget's Conservation Tasks

To investigate children's understanding of conservation, Piaget developed several tasks in which a substance—such as water in a glass, a ball of clay, or a line of coins—is transformed in its appearance, without changing the amount. In the conservation of number task, for example, children are shown two lines that have the same number of coins, and then watch as an interviewer spreads out the coins in one of the lines, which makes the line longer. Piaget showed that three to five year olds (in what he called the early "preoperational period") typically will say that the line of spaced coins has a different number and "has more" than the line of coins that are closer together. However, sometime between four and eight years of age, children develop the ability to *conserve quantity* over various perceptual transformations, or to recognize that the amount of a material can stay the same even as its appearance is transformed in some way. So, they are able to recognize that changing the *length* of the line does not change the *number* of coins, even though the change in spacing radically alters its appearance. Video examples of children completing Piaget's conservation tasks can easily be found online.

Typically younger children will say that there is more liquid in the taller, narrower glass. They explain that since the liquid level is higher, there must be more. Older children, on the other hand, will say that the amount of water in both glasses is still the same. Their verbal explanations show logical reasoning such as:

◆ *You didn't add or take away any water; you just poured it from one glass to the other.*

◆ *The second glass is taller, but the other glass is wider, so they are the same.*

◆ *If you pour water from the tall glass into the glass you took it from, the two glasses of the same size would be the same level again.*

Goldin-Meadow said that after years of showing videos of the Piagetian conservation tasks in child development courses she taught,

Piaget's Conservation Task

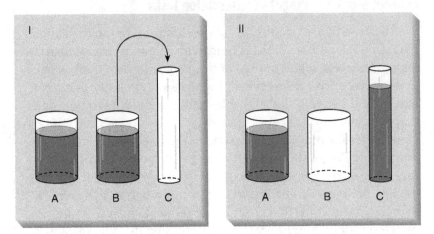

Figure 4.1 Piaget's liquid conservation task

she had an insight: "I always commented on the words that the children used [when they explained their thinking], but they also gestured like crazy, and nobody had ever mentioned it. So I started working with one of my students to code those gestures just to look at them."

She and her student, Ruth (Breckie) Church, videotaped 6 conservation tasks that they administered to 28 children between the ages of 5 and 8. For each task, they asked the children to make judgments and explain their reasoning. The researchers then created a coding system for analyzing children's speech separately from their gestures. When they compared the codes for each response, they found that some of the children used gestures that did not match the train of thought suggested by their speech.

As an example, on the liquid conservation task, a child might look at the short, wide glass and the tall, narrow glass, and say that there is more liquid in the tall glass because the liquid level in it is higher. However, that same child might simultaneously be using a gesture that indicates the glasses are of different widths. That is, he might make a "C" shape with one hand: first with the fingers closer to the thumb to indicate the narrow glass, and then with fingers farther from the thumb to indicate the wide glass (see Figure 4.2). Thus evidence from what this child *says* indicates that he is focused only on the height of the liquid in the two glasses: however, his *gestures* clearly indicate awareness of width as a second (and key) difference between the two

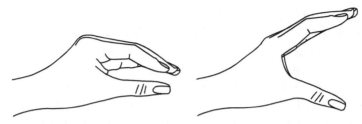

Figure 4.2 Children's gestures in Piaget's liquid conservation task. The left image is indicating a narrow glass, and the right image is indicating a wide glass

glasses. Goldin-Meadow and Church called this contrast between the understandings relayed in spoken word and gesture a **mismatch**.

Teacher Responses

◆ *I've seen this kind of "mismatch" happen many times with students, especially in estimation activities. Sometimes I use a "reference" jar with students to help give them something to compare to early in the year. For example, we'll have two identical jars and one will be filled with perhaps five to fifteen items, such as Unifix cubes. Students are told directly how many items are in the first jar. The second jar is then filled with double the amount of Unifix cubes, and students are asked to estimate how many it contains. I've heard students say that the second jar has only one or two more than the quantity in the first jar, even while their gestures make clear how aware they are of the very different height of the materials in the second jar. I think their gesture indicates a more accurate sense of the difference between the two amounts than they are able to convey in words.*

◆ *I see this kind of mismatching most often when children are switching between addition and subtraction. They will use the word "add" when "subtract" might be the better word, and they are clearly using their hands to demonstrate a "taking away" situation. I think they intuitively understand the inverse relationship between the two operations, but they are more comfortable with the idea of addition, so they default to "add."*

Mismatches as an Indicator of Readiness to Learn

Church and Goldin-Meadow's next step was to better understand why children exhibited these mismatches between speech and gesture when they explained their thinking. Church's dissertation work and subsequent publications with Goldin-Meadow established that, across the six conservation tasks, individual children typically produced a mixture of matches and mismatches; however, some children produced many more mismatches than others. The researchers wondered whether these children might be in a transitional stage in learning to conserve. They hypothesized that children who produced a lot of mismatches might be particularly ready to benefit from instruction about conservation.

To test this hypothesis, 52 children were given a pre-test of 6 conservation tasks and asked to explain their thinking, and researchers recorded their rate of gesture-speech mismatches versus matches. All children who could not yet conserve—regardless of their mismatching tendencies—were then given instruction in conservation, and then a post-test. The authors found that children who exhibited more mismatches than matches in the pre-test showed more improvement after instruction than those with more matches than mismatches. This finding indicated that, indeed, children who exhibit more mismatches are more ready to learn than children who do not.

According to Church and Goldin-Meadow, the results suggest that children move through three stages when learning about conservation (see Table 4.1). Before understanding conservation, their verbal responses are incorrect and tend to be matched by their explanatory gestures (e.g., indicating height of water level only). As their understanding of conservation begins to deepen, their verbal responses are usually still incorrect, but their gestures often do not match their verbal explanations (e.g., showing awareness of the width of the glass). Finally, when understanding of conservation has consolidated, their verbal responses are correct and are matched by their explanatory gestures (e.g., acknowledging differences in both height and width of the glasses). In other words, when moving from pre-learning to new understanding, a child's speech and gestures may move from mostly matched to mostly mismatched, and then back to mostly matched. Thus frequent mismatches may be a key indicator that a child is in a transitional stage in thinking about conservation.

The researchers' findings support the idea that cognitive struggle is highly productive. That is, struggling to reconcile two ideas calls for more active thinking than giving a rote response that one is "sure" is correct. As Church and Goldin-Meadow examined the data from their study, as well as from studies they completed on mathematical

Table 4.1 Three stages of learning conservation

| | **Time** | | |
	Pre-learning state	Transitional State	New understanding
Few speech-gesture mismatches	Both speech and gesture tend to suggest that the child believes that transformation of container, shape, or configuration will change quantity or amount.		Both speech and gesture tend to indicate that the child understands that transformation of container or shape does not change quantity. Understanding may have generalized as a principle.
Many speech-gesture mismatches		Different Information is conveyed in speech and gesture, suggesting that the child holds two different ideas simultaneously. Most often (but not always) the misconception or less abstract understanding is conveyed in speech, whereas the more advanced idea is conveyed in gesture.	

equivalence with older children, they saw evidence that children who didn't gesture, or whose gestures matched their verbal answers, usually assumed their verbal answer was correct and seldom questioned this assumption. In contrast, although the "mismatchers" often verbally expressed a wrong answer (probably the one they would have given without questioning it at all a year ago), their gestures indicated that they had begun to see the possibility that there was another way to consider the problem.

Teacher Responses

◆ *This finding makes me think about my English language learning students, how they often use gestures to get their meaning across. I think when I see a gesture/language mismatch there, I am often focused on the fact that the language is not correct. It makes me think: Have I missed opportunities to capitalize on what these students actually do understand?*

◆ *When I have my students look at images of up to eight items and tell me quickly how many there are without counting (subitizing), a majority of my students are very engaged. I do this by using cards with dots on them, arranged in structured ways that make it easy to see two sets of four dots, and asking children how many dots are on the card altogether. I can see that although they haven't ever studied the "double" fact "4 + 4" they have (or can build) knowledge that four objects and four objects put together makes eight. So they cannot say "4 + 4" but they can visualize the double. I feel like a visual number sense math talk like this gets at children's understanding of math concepts in a way that sort of circumvents what they can or cannot say. They don't have to be able to articulate it to understand it.*

◆ *I think with this age of children, it is natural that their gesture would be more closely tied to abstract concepts, while their language may not be there quite yet. It makes sense that the kind of thinking they can convey in gesture would outpace what they can explicitly say.*

Speech, Gesture, and Number

Goldin-Meadow found the same kind of difference between speech and gesture in work she conducted with colleagues on the development of children's early numerical understanding. Recall from Chapter 1 (Concept Box 1.1) that before children learn the cardinal principle (that the last number counted tells how many are in the set), they learn the cardinal meanings of the number words, in order, from one to four or five. That is, they learn "how many" objects the word "one" represents, then the word "two," and so on. It can take months to learn the meaning of each number word. One child might be able to link the correct number word to a set of one but not a set of two or above, whereas another might be able to do so for sets of one, two or three, but not four or above.

In studying children who were still learning these small number words, Goldin-Meadow and her colleagues hypothesized that children might understand something about the quantities, even if they couldn't connect them with the correct number words (e.g., if they see a set of four apples, they might have some understanding of its magnitude, even if they can't connect the word "four" to it). They wondered if such children might reveal some of this numerical knowledge through gestures.

To test this theory, they first identified children who did not yet know the cardinal principle (who were still in the process of learning the meanings of the numbers one through four). The researchers asked these children to look at cards displaying small sets of objects. At first, the children were asked to indicate the quantity of each set using the number words. In another activity, they were asked to hold up fingers to show the quantity.

Overall, the children's responses were correct more often when they were indicating set sizes using their *fingers* than when they were using *number words*. They were also more accurate using fingers than with number words when approximating higher numbers (five to ten). Further, sometimes children used both a word and a number gesture at the same time, and there were often mismatches (that is, the number word and gesture were different). In these cases, the gesture tended to be accurate more often than the word. In sum, children were able to show more knowledge about the quantities with number gestures than they could with number words.

Goldin-Meadow and colleagues theorized that using gestures might have been easier due to the one-to-one correspondence between the number of fingers and the number of objects shown on the card. Number names are arbitrary, cultural conventions and therefore may be harder to remember. The researchers also believe that, in this case, gesture might serve as an important bridge between a one-to-one understanding of amount and the cardinal amount concept toward which children are building. Recently Goldin-Meadow and colleagues have found that children who produce these gesture-speech mismatches on number tasks are more likely to profit from instruction, so here again a mismatch in speech and gesture may be an indicator of readiness-to-learn.

Teacher Responses

◆ *Recently I saw one student use his fingers to help another student understand the number word she was using. She said "four" and held up 10 fingers. He said, "No, four is like this" and held up four of his own fingers and then counted them out for her. I think of fingers as especially useful tools for representing small quantities, and it makes sense to me that children might be able to use this type of representation before they've got their number words right.*

◆ *The other day, Julian was the only child left at school at the end of the day, and he mentioned this, saying, "There's just me!" I asked him, "How many children are left?" and he said, "One." Then I asked how many PEOPLE there were altogether (implying he should count the two teachers as well). He looked at me puzzled, so I changed my question to "How many teachers are there?" He answered, "Two." Then I asked, "How many people are there altogether?" and he was completely silent, but slowly put up three fingers. I think he was mentally matching his fingers to the number of people.*

Gestures Aid Young Children's Mathematical Learning

More recently, Goldin-Meadow and her associates have confirmed not only that gestures provide useful clues to children's understanding, but also that they can be a significant aid to student learning. In one study with Raedy Ping, Goldin-Meadow provided instruction to five- to seven-year-olds about conservation. The instructor modeled conservation tasks and verbalized explanations as to why the amounts were still equal even after the transformation. For example, in the liquid conservation task, the instructor might have said, "One of the glasses is taller, and the other one is shorter. But the shorter glass is wider, and the taller glass is skinnier." In addition to the verbal explanation, some children also saw accompanying gestures. For example, when stating that one glass is taller and the other is shorter, the instructor made a gesture showing one hand held higher than the other; to show the difference in width, she made a C-shape with her hand, changing its width. The researchers found that children improved significantly more on the conservation task when the instruction they received included gestures.

Note that in the experiment above, the gestures used by the teacher were designed to reinforce what the teacher was saying.

To use Goldin-Meadow's terminology, the teachers' gestures and words *matched*. Thus they were conveying the same message through two modalities. However, further research that she conducted with Melissa Singer suggested that it can be more effective to use *mismatches* in instruction, particularly when the mismatch conveys *two different but correct ideas*—that is, when the teacher expresses one *correct* idea with words and simultaneously uses gestures to convey a second, also *correct* idea (see Concept Box 4.2). The researchers speculated that expressing both ideas verbally might be overwhelming to children, whereas when one idea is provided in speech and the second in gesture, one might enhance the child's understanding of the other.

Concept Box 4.2   Goldin-Meadow's Studies on Gesture and Mathematical Equivalence

Goldin-Meadow and her colleagues have conducted a series of studies examining ways to help children learn how to solve equivalence problems such as **6+4+5 = __+5**. The researchers first identified different ideas that children draw upon in order to solve the problems, as well as how children naturally express these ideas in language and in gesture. They then used these identified expressions (speech and gesture) in instruction, to see what types of input helped children learn how to solve the problems, such as in the study with Singer, above.

The following are examples of equivalence ideas and the gestures that suggest them:

1. *Equalizer*: The idea that both sides must be equal. This can be gestured with a flat palm sweeping first under the left side of the problem and then under the right.
2. *Add-subtract*: The strategy to add all numbers on one side and then subtract the number that is common on both sides (in the above example, the 5). This can be gestured by pointing at the 6, the 4, and the left 5, then producing a flick-away gesture near the right 5.

3. *Grouping*: The strategy to group the two non-common numbers (the 6 and the 4) and indicating that these should equal the number in the box. This can be gestured by making a "V" shape with two fingers under the two non-common numbers and then pointing to the box with the index finger.

In other studies, Goldin-Meadow and her colleagues found that students learn from gesturing themselves. In these studies, they had children attempt to solve problems, explaining their thinking using gesture, before they were given a lesson on how to solve the problems. In one study, the children were just told in general to use their hands to explain their thinking. In another study, children were told to produce a specific gesture. In both studies, the researchers found that children who were told to gesture learned more from the lesson than children who were not told to gesture. Why would gesturing help the children to learn? The researchers hypothesized that children may know some information implicitly, and that gesturing might help them access that information.

Teacher Responses

◆ *Certainly in math I use gestures, such as saying "How many in all?" and running my hand in a circle around all the materials that are meant to be associated with a specific set. I think my conscious use of gestures is always like this, where my gestures and my language match, and both convey the same message. I don't know if I am ever "mismatching" to convey two different but correct ideas at the same time.*

◆ *I consistently find that children are more engaged when they are asked to use gesture along with language, like in fingerplays. The children are able to grasp concepts—often related to number—more easily when they use gesture than when they don't. We also use some gesture in regard to shape, building the shape with our hands in the air or holding fingers for the number of sides. I have seen children call upon those movements as they use language to refer to the shapes, so I think making those gestures has been helpful to them.*

Conclusion

Goldin-Meadow's extensive research on gestures touches on the full spectrum of the complex role gesture plays in the teaching and learning dynamic. She and her colleagues have found that a learner's mismatch between words and gestures seems to signal readiness to develop new understanding; they have also found that when a teacher matches words and gestures, or when the teacher uses gestures that provide additional insight that is different from the words alone, learning is enhanced. They have also found that having children gesture themselves can help them learn.

Teachers Respond to the Research

The teachers in our seminar found the research on gesture very relevant; one even said, "This validates what I've been doing all my life—lots of people tease me because I gesture so much, but this work helps me see its value." Given that most of our seminar teachers are working in schools that feature a wide variety of home language situations and that Spanish is the first language for three of them, it isn't surprising that many teachers' questions and comments were about the relationship between language learning and gesture. Teachers were also interested, of course, in how they could use gesture or an awareness of it more effectively in the classroom.

Gesture and English Language Learners

In talking about the use of gesture in their classrooms, the teachers had a lot to say about the language problems their students were experiencing as second language learners. They made remarks such as, "I think he had the idea, but he didn't have the words in English." Two of their stories are below:

> ◆ *I have become more aware of the importance of using gestures, especially in my situation, in which my students learn math in their second language. I had an experience in which children had to solve a two-step math word problem and when they first tried, they just added numbers randomly. As we read it again and again, breaking down the pieces of information one by one, and we included gestures to explain it, students became able to identify the steps they had to take to solve the problem.*

◆   *I keep thinking of my student Miguel whose home language is*
    Spanish. When I ask him "How many hearts did you draw?," he
    counts "one, two, three, four," although there are three hearts. But
    when I ask him to "show me" with his fingers, he can hold up just
    three. So he is able to show three with his fingers accurately but
    can't coordinate this with the counting procedure and words.

What is the role of gesture in second language learning, and how does it relate to gesture as an aid to developing conceptual understanding of math?

Susan Goldin-Meadow's Response

As the research presented in this chapter demonstrates, gesture is a powerful communicator and can sometimes be a better reflection of understanding than spoken language alone. In the first example above, where gesture helps English learners understand a word problem, gesture is providing an additional channel of information about what is occurring in the situation. When children randomly add numbers, it is because they do not yet understand the relationships between the numbers as the story describes them; in this case, gesture helped make the situation described in English words clearer.

There is a common misconception about math—that it is somehow not dependent upon language. In fact, many math researchers believe we could not have a number system at all without language. More importantly, mathematics has to be learned within meaningful contexts. Math only makes sense because of the ways it represents our real experiences. So for English learners who are learning to think mathematically in English, it is especially important to take the time to make sure everyone understands "the problem." Gesture can clearly be a useful tool to accomplish this.

The second example provides a clear window into the math thinking of a young English learner. Miguel knows many things: he knows that when asked "how many," he should implement a counting procedure; he knows the number words up to four and how to say them in the right order; and, importantly, he has and can demonstrate a conceptual understanding of "three-ness." By giving him a chance to express his thinking with his hands, Miguel's teacher learned about what he knows, and more importantly, what he still needs to work on: establishing one-to-one correspondence in his counting procedure so he can connect counting to cardinal amount. Gesture is a powerful additional indicator of children's mathematical thinking, and teachers of emergent bilingual students can use it to help them.

Gesture and Total Physical Response

Several teachers mentioned Total Physical Response (TPR), a teaching strategy they have used with English language learners (ELLs). In this technique, teachers and students connect vocabulary or concepts to a specific gesture or an action. The gesture or action provides an additional cue to help ELLs (and other students as well) remember the word's meaning.

◆ *TPR taught me to gesture deliberately when I introduce new vocabulary words. Often, we create gestures together as a class. For example, we had a unit on equality, and were discussing segregation—a very abstract idea! I had students work with me to craft gestures that represented the meaning of the word as they understood it.*

◆ *When using TPR, for addition, I represent the first addend on one hand and represent the second addend with the other. Then I put my hands together for them to see how two sets come together as part of the addition process. For subtraction, I start with my hands together to represent the total as I label the idea of total, and then take one hand away to show taking away one set of numbers to find what remains.*

What are the differences and similarities between gesture consciously used as an additional form of representation, as with TPR, and the spontaneous gestures you commonly study?

Susan Goldin-Meadow's Response

I don't know much about TPR, but it sounds like gestures are used to provide an additional channel of information, explicitly matched to what is being said. It makes sense that this would be a good way to help children become familiar with English words, including math words. It also seems like creating gestures together to accompany new words and ideas would be a very powerful mechanism for learning!

Both TPR and unconscious gesturing use spoken words and gestures in concert so that the meaning is communicated in two ways simultaneously. However, the unconscious gestures may convey more complexity than would be useful in the TPR technique, which is intentionally reinforcing the match between word and gesture. Unconscious gesturing, as we have seen, sometimes conveys different additional information not found in speech.

My research on spontaneous, unconscious gestures has often led me to explore the importance of *mismatches*. I am particularly interested in cases when a mismatch is an indication that thinking is shifting, as when a child is not able to conserve verbally but seems to be aware of another way to think about the problem. Other times, as in my research on mathematical equivalence (see Concept Box 4.2), a mismatch is a way to express two different but correct ways of thinking simultaneously. Because TPR is focused on a more explicit match between speech and gesture, it may not convey as much information as unconscious gesturing can. But it seems to convey information in a very powerful way, particularly for certain learners—we would need more research to find out! Perhaps we could even get ideas for the movements used in TPR from the spontaneous gestures that teachers (and students) produce.

Gesture and Clarification

In addition to questions about gesture and second language learning, teachers began to think about their own and other adults' unconscious use of gesture. Many of their comments and questions were about the kind of communicative contexts that are more likely to bring about its use.

◆ *I am seeing that gesture is a valuable piece of a teaching and learning environment, and I'm not sure how much the children in my class are using it. I know that I can use it myself more, but I wonder what kind of situations might prompt the children to use gesture.*

◆ *After reading this chapter, I began to notice gesture among my peers. In a recent meeting, it seemed to me that other teachers and administrators were using gesture when they felt particularly passionate about what they were thinking. Gesture was especially common when someone was trying to convey something a second time—that is, they seemed to feel the first time they talked about it, they were not quite understood, so they were trying again.*

When are children most likely to use gesture? Does it often occur when they are trying to clarify a verbal explanation, or "make a point?"

Susan Goldin-Meadow's Response

Gesture that accompanies speech is definitely an indication that the speaker is thinking about what she is saying and intends to communicate. And certainly, gesture is sometimes motivated (among sophisticated communicators) by a sense that words are not enough to convey meaning without them, or that the need for effective understanding is urgent, which may be felt when a listener appears confused or unconvinced.

Anecdotally, we have seen that gestures are likely to accompany speech when something must be "re-said" because it was not understood the first time. It is not clear, however, how sophisticated an awareness of other people's minds is necessary to motivate gesture in these ways. Babies point to direct the attention of others, but that is not quite the same as using gesture as a response to confusion in the recipient of our message.

Probably the most important thing is to be sure they have many chances to try to make themselves understood. As children become more sophisticated communicators, they need moments where an adult "gives them the floor" and not only asks what they think, but also asks why they think it—in other words, the adult asks them to explain their thinking. As children get older, it will be possible for them to be listeners for each other, particularly if the conversations are structured for them by a thoughtful adult. Representing their thinking for the understanding of others is obviously a powerful learning experience, regardless of whether they gesture as part of it or not. But clearly, without a listener and something interesting to try to convey, there is no need for gesture, although we do have evidence that blind people gesture when talking to other blind people, suggesting that gesture can be for the self.

Gesture and Development

Teachers also had questions about whether there was a developmental trajectory for gesture.

◆ *I think some of my students are using more gesture than others, and I am wondering why. Should I be concerned? Is there something I can do to affect this or is it something that has to develop on its own?*

◆ *In trying to think about when and where I see children using unconscious gesture, I find myself thinking more about my older students. This is something I think I see more among my more verbal children, whereas younger children use gesture more deliberately, perhaps to direct others' attention.*

Is there a developmental trajectory for gesture that can be described? Does it seem to develop alongside language in some predictable way? Are there other factors that influence whether a child might gesture more or less? Could instruction in gesturing be helpful?

Susan Goldin-Meadow's Response

As I mentioned above, babies use pointing, often before they have any words at all. Pointing is a particularly interesting gesture, both because it has a clear meaning that can be understood based simply on context and without accompanying language ("there," or "look there," or "that"), and because, unlike many later-developing gestures, it has a specific referent in the world: an object, person, or place to whom the "speaker" wants to direct the "listener's" attention. In these ways, we might consider pointing a "less abstract" form of gesture. In early childhood, we see children begin to use their fingers to represent cardinal amount—the "three-ness" of three depicted by holding up three fingers, for example. Cardinal meaning is a very abstract concept itself, but this gesture is, again, a very specific, unambiguous gesture that requires little verbal explanation.

It's clear that at some point, gestures become a bit more abstract. In the conservation tasks we have used in our studies, when children's explanations of their thinking are "mismatching," their gestures have a particularly spatial function, as they provide a means of describing physical attributes, such as the width of a glass. Here again there is a physical referent, and the gesture, at least within the context of the experience, conveys a lot of specific information on its own. However, the ability to mismatch itself—that is, to say one thing with words and another with hands—suggests complexity of thought that probably doesn't exist earlier in development. It's also true that something like mismatch does happen very early in development. For example, when a one-word child says "mommy" while pointing at a cup to indicate that it's mommy's cup, she is conveying one idea in speech and another in gesture, which is technically a mismatch—so mismatch can happen at a young age. And, interestingly, these types of early "mismatches" predict the onset of two-word speech in toddlers ("mommy cup").

Eventually, of course, gestures are used simultaneously with speech to provide emphasis, to allude to the co-existence of differing ideas, to mark time or sequence, and so on. In these cases, the ideas that gestures represent—relative importance, perspective, and the passing of time—are quite abstract, with little physical manifestation that can be pointed to as a referent. We do not have thorough enough research at this point to document this progression with certainty, but we see that it exists. Regarding the amount of gesture a child uses, we simply do not know what contributes to these individual differences, or even if great differences exist. I suspect that rate of gesturing varies within a person across contexts and tasks—we all gesture more when we're thinking hard about a problem. But there may be a genetic predisposition to gesture (I doubt it) or a sensitivity to gestures used by adults (more likely), or it may be a function of how much communication of any kind is in the child's environment or perhaps directed to the child. Most likely, it is some combination of all of these factors, and perhaps others that we are simply not yet aware of.

I think the kind of deliberate use of "signs" some teachers have described in this chapter sounds like a really positive use of gesture, and we know from our research that children who were encouraged to use gesture to explain their thinking learned more. I'd say that the best thing to do would be to use it yourself, use it deliberately in ways that make sense, and most importantly, encourage its use by children. It's not clear whether you can improve the gesturing itself (or even what it means to improve gesturing), but the gesture may improve children's learning.

Using Gesture to Convey Two Different Ideas When Teaching

Our seminar teachers were interested to become more reflective about their own use of gesture. In particular, they wanted more information about their own "mismatches"—when would the use of gesture to include a second message be helpful, and when might it cause confusion in students?

- *I would like more information on the idea of there being "mismatches" in instruction, such as conveying one idea with words and using gestures to convey a second, correct idea.*

- *I wonder where the line is between a gesture that effectively shows the same concept in a different way and one that confuses children. Isn't it sometimes more important that a single idea is emphasized?*

Susan Goldin-Meadow's Response

Given what we do know, and also how much about gesture we still do not understand, the best thing for teachers to do is to be aware of their use of gesture, and to pay attention to what seems to be helpful to children and what might be confusing. Most often, gestures are incidental in our experiences as learners—they are not explained by the teacher, but simply given in context without comment. This characteristic is both something that makes them powerful, and something that makes them risky. Awareness, reflection, and thoughtful use will help a teacher avoid confusing children.

Teachers' Ideas for Classroom Practice

Based on their understanding of the research, teachers had a lot to say about how an awareness of gesture can be thoughtfully used in the classroom. Below, we summarize some of the more powerful of their ideas.

Use Gesture Deliberately in the Classroom

- *I think, as a preschool teacher, I look for as many ways as possible to connect with the child: visual, auditory, and kinesthetic. I was taught that we need to give children all these experiences because in a group you have all these types of learners. So I'm connecting gesture with kinesthetic learning.*

- *Talking about gesture makes me think about how I often have students act out or draw a word problem before they try to solve it. It seems like gesture is one more way students can represent, and perhaps develop, their understanding.*

- *We use a variety of deliberate gestures, not only for math concepts, but also for things like "me too," "stop," "sit down," and "finished." Our class also has a secret code for "quiet" and we are continuing to develop signs as the children decide they are needed.*

◆ *Asking a five-year-old to show you what they mean non-verbally can help you understand their thinking in more depth.*

For the most part, early childhood teachers excel at providing a learning environment that incorporates physical movement. Teachers of young children know that they must manage and should plan for different levels of activity at different points in the day. Learning experiences where children dance or move in patterned ways are a common element of many preschool and kindergarten classrooms, and recess and free play are designed to—among other things—allow children greater physical autonomy than is possible during circle time or at the snack table. Early childhood "lessons" reflect these understandings when they incorporate children themselves into an activity; by acting out Goldilocks on the rug, for example; or doing a "people sort" where children with zippers on their clothes stand in one hula hoop and children with no zippers stand in another. Teachers in our seminar made a clear connection between gesture use and awareness of the value of consciously used kinesthetic activities.

On the other hand, the teachers were clear that their own use of gesture could be more conscious and deliberate. They noted its ability to provide additional information when children are learning a new word. Like many instructional strategies that are helpful for ELLs, this one is excellent for all children in the classroom. Further, some teachers are using deliberate, planful gesture to communicate beyond instances of challenging vocabulary. When the gesture for "quiet" is used by the teacher, and then mimicked by the students as they become aware of it, it becomes a silent yet participatory way for children to help each other become quiet. Their attention is gathered by the teacher and they have a more active role than "sitting down quietly" when they can make the gesture themselves to help everything along. It's a way of connecting with their teacher without talk.

Train Yourself to Watch for Children's Gestures (and Mismatches)

◆ *Before reading this, I did think that using gestures to teach students concepts or words could be helpful. But I didn't make the effort to look for gestures that students may be using. I think I do see students using both verbal and non-verbal skills, but my focus tends to be on the verbal.*

- ◆ *I have not really paid attention to children's gestures, and particularly have not noticed when gestures and speech mismatch. I do know there is a transitional point where a student is beginning to get a concept, and I am usually watching for clues to this; being on the lookout for mismatches may help me spot those who are ready to learn.*

- ◆ *I have always paid more attention to gesture from the teaching perspective rather than how the students are using it. I always ask myself: am I using gesture to help them understand this concept? This research makes me pay more attention to how children are using gesture to explain their thinking.*

- ◆ *This reminds me of when we were talking about where we live, and Emiliano came up to me and said, "I here" and pointed up, and added "she there" while pointing down. He's talking about the apartment building his family shares with his grandma, and saying, "I live above her." But he doesn't have the language to express it. To me, that use of gesture is replacing the words he doesn't have—it's not that he doesn't understand the concept. So by paying attention to his words **and** his gestures, I'm getting all the information.*

Learning to pay more attention to children's gestures is not easy. There is so much going on in the early childhood classroom that paying close attention to how children move their hands while they speak may be difficult to accomplish. One recommendation is to select a circle time or other occasion when you expect children to explain their thinking and to videotape it. It can be as simple as having another adult use a cell phone to focus on children's statements and gestures. Watching video such as this together can help you and your teaching colleagues become aware of different types of gesture. If, away from the busy classroom, you are able to think carefully about gestures' meanings—and notice which children are using them and when—they will become easier to spot in the middle of a hectic day.

Important Impact of Finger Use in Representing Number

- ◆ *The holding up of fingers to indicate quantity seems to me to be more of a matching activity than the verbal labeling of the set with number names. However, at some point, it seems like the fingers become sort of symbolic themselves—we just know that a hand held up with one's thumb down is "four".*

◆ *When I ask children how many items are in a set of four or five, and they have not mastered the skills and knowledge to count out loud and tag the objects, I often see them slowly put up their fingers. I think the children are using their fingers to match the items in one-to-one correspondence.*

◆ *I have also wanted to push myself to work with the children on representing quantities with different types of "formations" on fingers—so working on composing and decomposing numbers by representing five on two hands instead of one, for example.*

It is clear from this chapter that fingers as representations of small quantities are very special gestures. As Goldin-Meadow herself points out, fingers can represent the meaning of the quantities—the "three-ness" of three—in a way that the words ("three") and numerals ("3") never can. This means children have a built-in tool for telling you how they are thinking about small quantities that doesn't rely on what they are able to say! This tool is with them everywhere: on the playground, in line for the restroom, at the playhouse, at the snack table. Fingers are a powerful, flexible, and convenient mechanism for working a little bit of math into many activities.

It's also true, as a teacher above points out, that because we have two hands, we have multiple ways to express each number. We can hold up five fingers on one hand, or we can show two on the right and three on the left. Children find it fascinating that there are different ways to show "five-ness" and will want to explore every combination that makes five that they can find, once they understand the general principle. Playing "show me five" can be a great way to excuse children from the rug a few at a time, or keep everyone entertained while waiting for the bathroom. The key is to narrate and describe what children do, as in "Oh, I see you are showing four on one hand and one on the other . . . that's five too!," helping other children make the connections.

Providing Opportunities for Students to Explain Their Thinking

◆ *This research made clear to me the importance of allowing students to come up with their own ways of explaining things. That's the only way you can catch misunderstandings as they are happening, and since children in pre-K are limited in how much they can explain using paper and pencil—or even words—gesture seems like a natural way for them to demonstrate what they know and are thinking about.*

◆ *My own experience of math learning had very little talking in it, and what talking there was mostly done by the teacher! Seeing that gesture is so connected to mathematics makes me even more sure how important it is for students to have the chance to communicate with me and with other students about their own math thinking. If I don't make it possible, it won't happen.*

◆ *Goldin-Meadow believes that when you use gesture to explain your thinking, you end up understanding your own thinking better. And I think that makes sense—it makes sense intuitively that if you're struggling with explaining something, and you use your hands to gesture, it helps you. It helps not just your listener, but it helps you! Between language and gesture, I think we're using both to communicate.*

As we have seen, gesture is a very powerful communicator, and not just for mathematics. It's also true that gestures—especially unconscious gestures—are likely to accompany our speech when we are struggling to communicate in words. This means, if children are to gesture, they must have opportunities to attempt to make themselves understood.

In traditional mathematics classes, children explaining their thinking was a rarity. The problem was presented, the teacher demonstrated how to solve it and explained the thinking herself, and then students silently practiced the problem type, demonstrating use of a single new strategy or procedure over and over on paper. As math educators, we have become aware how valuable it is to spend time talking together about thinking. This proves a much more powerful mechanism for generating understanding among more students, and helps to create flexibility of thought around mathematics. Students who listen to and talk about multiple ways to solve the same problem are much more likely to be able to apply strategies in useful ways, even when it is not obvious that the strategy is required.

It is also the case that this kind of "math talk" creates multiple opportunities for gesture use among children. Explaining one's thinking is never easy to do—it requires anticipating the knowledge of someone else in complicated ways. If we give children opportunities to struggle with this process of clarifying their own thoughts so they can be understood by someone else, they will be more likely to develop as fluent thinkers. They will have practice turning their thoughts into words at a more challenging level and will learn what kinds of words make them more likely to be and feel understood. And gesture will be part of supporting this very meta-cognitive task, whether in math or in some other topic.

The Bottom Line

The idea that learners should be active agents in constructing their understanding goes back to Piaget–Susan Goldin-Meadow's first mentor. However, her research has added a significant new element to this field of study—the idea that *gesture* can play an important role in constructing understanding. She has shown that teachers obtain powerful clues about what is going on in a child's mind by paying attention to gestures, looking as carefully for those that don't match their words as well as those that do. Furthermore, teachers who support their explanations or demonstrations with their own gestures enhance their students' learning.

The beauty of gestures is that they aren't a code—they are spontaneous and often used unconsciously. There isn't a script to follow about the correct way to use or interpret them. However, they are always meaningful—and are an essential feature of how we express ourselves—especially when we are trying to communicate something that can't be, or is difficult to be, reduced to words. Teachers know that a strong signal that children understand something is that they can put it into their own words, perhaps using an example that makes particular sense to them. Goldin-Meadow's research indicates that gestures can similarly provide insight into a child's understanding.

Key Research Studies Discussed

Broaders, S., Cook, S. W., Mitchell, Z., and Goldin-Meadow, S. (2007). Making children gesture reveals implicit knowledge and leads to learning. *Journal of Experimental Psychology: General, 136*(4), 539–550. doi:10.1037/0096–3445.135.4.539

Church, R. B., and Goldin-Meadow, S. (1986). The mismatch between gesture and speech as an index of transitional knowledge. *Cognition, 23*, 43–71.

Goldin-Meadow, S. (2009). How gesture promotes learning throughout childhood. *Child Development Perspectives, 3*, 106–111.

Goldin-Meadow, S., and Singer, M. A. (2003). From children's hands to adults' ears: Gesture's role in the learning process. *Developmental Psychology, 39*(3), 509–520.

Novack, R. B, Congdon, E. L., Hemani-Lopez, N., and Goldin-Meadow, S. (2014). From action to abstraction: Using the hands to learn math. *Psychological Science, 25*(4), 903–910. doi:10.1177/0956797613518351

Perry, M., Church, R. B., and Goldin-Meadow, S. (1992). Is gesture-speech mismatch a general index of transitional knowledge? *Cognitive Development, 7*(1), 109–122.

Ping, R., and Goldin-Meadow, S. (2008). Hands in the air: Using ung-rounded iconic gestures to teach children conservation of quantity. *Developmental Psychology, 44*(5), 1277. doi:10.1037/0012–1649.44.5.1277

5

Variability in Children's Mathematical Thinking and Learning

Laura Grandau and Rebeca Itzkowich, with Robert Siegler

Understanding how young children think and how learning happens is an exciting but complicated endeavor. Many educators are aware of the work of the developmental psychologist Jean Piaget, who dedicated much of his research to identifying the fundamental nature of children's thinking at particular ages. Piaget's work and his theory about four universal stages of cognitive development (*Sensorimotor*, *Preoperational*, *Concrete Operational*, and *Formal Operational*) transformed the way we think about childhood and development. Although in many ways the current field of cognitive psychology has continued to follow Piaget's lead since his death in 1980, there have also been challenges and advances that have taken his work deeper and pushed in new directions. One such path was taken by cognitive psychologists who were unsatisfied with Piaget's focus on sharp stages of development. They believed that reasoning develops more fluidly, and were interested in understanding how thinking unfolds, how children acquire and use new information and strategies, and how change and learning can be followed on the micro-level.

In this chapter, we focus on one of these researchers, Robert S. Siegler, Professor of Cognitive Psychology at Carnegie Mellon University. For decades, Siegler has studied children's learning and changes in children's thinking, particularly as these topics relate to mathematics. He takes a "zoomed in" perspective—gathering a lot of detailed information over a period of time—to understand gradually changing characteristics in children's thinking. Along with important contributions to mathematics education, Siegler's methods for understanding change and development have had great impact on what we know about how learning happens. In the sections that follow, we focus on three interconnected areas of his work, all related to mathematics, and all that expand on Piaget's work: cognitive variability, the path of children's learning, and the value of working with multiple strategies. Understanding these ideas provides perspective and possibility for our work with young children.

Background

Siegler told us that he has always been fascinated by change. He says that his favorite subject in school was history, and the part of it he liked best was thinking about how the pasts of different countries influenced their presents and their likely futures. As a child, he was also interested in mathematical problem solving. He was particularly interested in the statistics on the back of baseball cards, and would use that information to identify which teams were most likely to win the World Series.

When Siegler began his research as a graduate student, Piaget's theory of development was the dominant approach to cognitive development. While Siegler believed that Piaget was a genius at coming up with tasks that reveal children's understanding of concepts, he did not believe Piaget's theory was totally on target. Siegler's work set out to go deeper and use different methods—to understand *how* and *why* certain ways of thinking emerge. Much of his work focused on mathematical thinking because, as he told us, the subject had always interested him, and because he believes that it has an important role in children's outcomes. In order to assess how and why children's thinking develops, Siegler uses what is called a *microgenetic* research approach (see Concept Box 5.1).

Concept Box 5.1   The Microgenetic Approach to Studying Cognitive Development

The microgenetic approach is a research approach that aims to shed light on the process of change. It grew out of work by Lev Vygotsky and others as early as the 1920s. According to Siegler, any method aimed at studying development and change must examine changes *while they are occurring*. Practically speaking, he says, "It is extremely difficult to accurately infer how a change occurred by comparing behavior before and after the change. Looking in on change in real time is critical." This is the goal of the microgenetic approach.

Siegler says that microgenetic methods have at least two key characteristics: 1) subjects are observed, and usually videotaped, over an extended period of time; and 2) their learning is subjected to intensive trial-by-trial analysis, with the goal of inferring processes that give rise to change. Microgenetic studies can involve interactions with child subjects that include questions, feedback, and explanation directed at the child. For example, while observing a child solving a problem, the researcher might ask, "How did you know that?" or say, "Yes, that's right. You do need two more to get to eight." During the intensive observations involved in this method, researchers are focused on children's overt behaviors as well as their explanations of their capabilities, confusions, ideas, and decisions. According to Siegler, the microgenetic approach can reveal the steps and circumstances that precede a change, the change itself, and how change might occur beyond its initial context.

What the Research Says

Children's Thinking and Strategy Use Is Highly Variable

In 1982, Siegler and a colleague at Carnegie Mellon University, Mitch Robinson, led a project designed to investigate conceptual understandings in young children. Different from Piaget's approach, the goal of this project was to examine children's performance on a variety of tasks related to the same concept, and to better understand the representations and processes children use to complete the different tasks. These researchers hoped that in the end, they could produce a model that characterized the ways that children think about a given conceptual domain.

The concept that the researchers selected for their study was number. They assessed three, four, and five year olds' competence in counting, magnitude comparison, number conservation, and addition. In the course of their work the researchers noticed many interesting patterns and behaviors, especially in the children's responses to the addition problems. As Siegler noted, "Although the addition experiment was planned as only one part of the larger whole, the results that it yielded were sufficiently interesting that they became the center of my research for several years to follow."

A closer look at this research tells the story. In this study, Siegler and Robinson videotaped individual four- and five-year-old students responding to addition problems over the course of six one-on-one sessions with a researcher. In these sessions, the researchers established a particular problem context: "You have m oranges, and I'm going to give you n to add to your pile. How many do you have altogether?" They gave this problem using the number combinations listed in Figure 5.1, presenting each problem twice over the six sessions. They did not give the children feedback, except to assure them periodically that they were doing well. For each problem, the researchers recorded whether the children answered it correctly or not, the strategy that they observed them using, the length of time it took to solve the problem, and for incorrect answers, how far off they were from the correct number.

Overall, Siegler and Robinson found that four-year-olds were correct on 66% of the addition problems, and five-year-olds were correct on 79%. While this may not seem surprising, specific attributes of

```
1+1; 1+2; 1+3; 1+4; 1+5
2+1; 2+2; 2+3; 2+4; 2+5
3+1; 3+2; 3+3; 3+4; 3+5
4+1; 4+2; 4+3; 4+4; 4+5
5+1; 5+2; 5+3; 5+4; 5+5
```

Figure 5.1 Number combinations for the "oranges" problem

particular problems and a variety of solution strategies became salient. Together they demonstrated that a considerable range of mathematical thinking, understanding, and strategy use exists at the preschool age.

The researchers observed four types of strategies that children used when solving the problems: Counting Fingers, Fingers, Counting, and No Visible Strategy. These are described in Table 5.1. Findings related to these arithmetic strategies are shown in Table 5.2 (data from Siegler & Robinson, 1982). As is evident, a variety of strategies were used, and different strategies were associated with longer and shorter solution times and degrees of accuracy. For example, "counting fingers" took the longest but was among the two most accurate strategies. "No visible strategy" was the fastest but was not as accurate.

The table gives an overall picture of the strategies used; however, one of the most interesting findings was the *variability* in the strategies used by individual children. The researchers observed that children did not consistently use just one strategy (i.e., a child typically did not only use a counting fingers strategy or only a counting strategy). Rather, children used a *mix* of strategies. The researchers observed that 80% of children used multiple strategies: 23% used two strategies, 30% used three strategies, and 27% used four strategies. Further, in over one-third of the pairs of trials for a given problem, the same child solved the same problem using two different strategies. This was an important finding. Prior to this, researchers had described the development of

Table 5.1 Addition strategies observed in Siegler and Robinson's study

Strategy	Description
Counting fingers	Child puts up fingers on one hand, puts up fingers on other hand, then counts the two sets.
Fingers	Child puts up fingers as in counting strategy above, but shows no evidence of counting them before answering.
Counting	Child counts aloud from 1 without any visible referent.
No visible strategy	This is a catch-all category for approaches that did not exhibit any visible or audible behaviors that seemed related to the addition process. Although the researchers could not be sure of what children were doing to solve the problems, this category theoretically captured instances of *retrieval*, or instances when the children remembered the answer.

Table 5.2 Findings regarding different strategies used in Siegler and Robinson's study

Strategy	Trials on which strategy was used (%)	Mean solution time (seconds)	Correct answers (%)	Errors on which answer was within one of correct sum (%)
Counting fingers	15	14.0	87	70
Fingers	13	6.6	89	80
Counting	8	9.0	54	44
No visible strategy	64	4.0	66	41

early mathematical thinking as a progression through a sequence of strategies. In other words, children first use strategy A, then progress to strategy B, then strategy C, and so on. If this were the case, children should only have been using one strategy at any given time.

Teacher Responses

◆ *I think it would be very helpful to talk to other preschool teachers about the specific strategies they are teaching and seeing in the classroom. I recognize that strategies are happening in my preschool classroom, but I don't often name them or think about how they are developing.*

Equally striking to the researchers was the way that *types* of problems were related to performance and strategy use. For example, they noted that the size of the sum and the size of the addend (meaning the second number, or the additional oranges given in the problem) affected rates. They also noticed that children used the visible strategies, as the researchers called them (counting fingers, fingers, and counting), more often in the more difficult problems, and used no visible strategy in the easier problems. Thus, children seemed to be adaptively selecting different strategies depending on the difficulty of the item.

Follow-up studies by Siegler and other researchers also documented variability in the ways young students use strategies when stacking blocks, telling time, working number conservation problems, and solving subtraction problems. About these findings, Siegler (2007) writes, "Children's thinking is far more variable than has usually been recognized. . . . Recognizing this variability is important not only for accurately describing development but also for understanding cognitive change."

Teacher Responses

- ◆ *I was surprised by this, honestly. I haven't seen students using a mix of strategies, or at least not what I thought was a mix of strategies. Instead, what I felt I was seeing often was a student struggling with one strategy and trying repeatedly to work out a problem using that single strategy. Now it occurs to me that perhaps either I wasn't recognizing the use of multiple strategies, or students were only given the time or opportunity to demonstrate the use of one strategy at any point in time.*

- ◆ *This research made me wonder if I am teaching my students enough strategies. How do I know if they understand the strategies I'm teaching? Are they using them effectively? Can I identify the similarities and differences in the strategies they are using?*

Children's Learning Does Not Occur in a Step-Like or Linear Progression

Having documented that children possess multiple ways of thinking at any one time, Siegler and colleagues decided to look more carefully at children's strategy use across time. When they re-examined the addition data from the study described above, they found that children often used more than one strategy in two sessions that were close to one another. And, contrary to what one might expect, the use of two different strategies for the same problem did not always—or even often—reflect progress from the earlier to the later session. For example, a child could use a more advanced strategy such as accurate retrieval (a type of "no visible strategy") to solve a problem, but in a later session use fingers to solve the same problem. This suggested that children were not always moving from less advanced to more advanced strategies.

In this and other studies, Siegler began to examine children's patterns of strategy use across time. Siegler and his team kept track of the frequencies of strategy use at the different sessions and found they would change over time. Children would begin to use some strategies more and some less; they would construct new strategies and abandon old ones. Based on these findings, Siegler proposed a new way of thinking about how change occurs called the *Overlapping Waves Model*.

Figure 5.2 displays both the traditional perspective on children's learning (left side) and Siegler's overlapping waves theory (right side). The depiction on the left side shows development and change occurring during relatively brief transitional periods ranging from when the child "doesn't have" the competency to when the child "has" it. This model shows a simple, linear path, and is sometimes called the "staircase" progression.

On the right side of Figure 5.2, development is shown as involving changes in the frequency of strategy use. Over a set period of time, children start to use some problem-solving strategies less frequently (see Strategy 1), others more frequently (see Strategy 5), and some more frequently and then less frequently (Strategy 2). They discover new strategies (Strategies 3 and 5), and stop using older strategies (Strategy 1; Siegler, 2005). The depiction suggests that in learning, children do not progress from one approach to a second approach and then to a third, like the traditional model suggests. Instead, development involves changes in the frequency with which particular strategies are used over time.

The Overlapping Waves Model also suggests another idea that was new at the time—that children can have multiple ways of thinking about ideas for prolonged periods. According to the model, children do not first think in one way consistently, and later think in another way consistently. Rather, at any given time they have multiple ways of thinking and approaching problems.

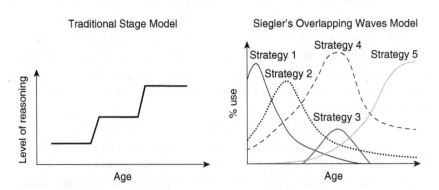

Figure 5.2 Schematic depictions of change

Teacher Responses

◆ *I thought it was interesting that researchers previously thought that children's early mathematical thinking progressed through stages instead of adapting a strategy to meet their needs at any given time. In my experience, students pull out and repack strategies on a daily basis. They are very fluid in their thinking. Anything from the mood they are in, to the students they are working with, can dictate which strategy they activate on any given occasion.*

◆ *What really spoke to me about the idea here is that "children can have multiple ways of thinking about ideas for prolonged periods." I'm thinking about this idea and assessment. Testing is a snapshot of how a child is thinking at a particular point in time rather that a true measure of what a child can do. I am interested in finding out more about ways a young child can demonstrate he knows something, and how I can know more about his thinking process.*

Children Derive Considerable Advantages From Using Multiple Strategies

In another study, Siegler (1995) demonstrated a third powerful idea about strategy use: the idea that children *derive advantages from using multiple strategies.*

In this study, broadly designed to illustrate the types of information that microgenetic methods can yield, Siegler examined four-and-a-half to six-year-old children's performance and thinking on the classic Piagetian "conservation of number" task. In the basic version of this task, children are presented with two parallel rows of objects where each object in the first row is aligned with an object in the second row. Children are asked whether one row has more objects or whether they have the same number of objects. Once they determine that the two rows have the same number of objects, the experimenter spreads out the objects in one of the rows and asks if the two rows now have the same number or if one has more. Piaget found that until age six or seven, children often say that the row that is spread out has more objects because it is longer.

In this study, children were given versions of the conservation-of-number task over eight sessions. Each time, children were shown the two equal rows aligned in one-to-one correspondence. Then, one of the rows was transformed. Transformations could occur in two important ways: quantitatively and/or spatially. Quantitative transformations included *adding* an item to a row or *subtracting* an item. Rows could also remain the same quantity (neither adding nor subtracting an item). Spatial transformations included *lengthening* a row, *shortening* a row, or moving items *back and forth so they were the same length as before*. These six types of problems are represented in Table 5.3.

The researchers used the first four sessions to determine whether the children had already mastered number conservation. In these "pre-test" sessions, children were presented with 12 conservation trials. Half involved rows of 2, 3, or 4 items, and the other half involved rows of 7, 8, or 9 items. On trials in the pretest condition, children were not given any feedback, except the occasional "good job" because they were "trying hard." The pretest procedure did not produce learning—no training was provided.

Next, the 45 (out of 97) children who did not demonstrate mastery on the pretest were given four additional sessions in which they received "training" on the tasks. Training sessions focused on conservation tasks using only large sets of items (7, 8, or 9 items in each row) and involved feedback and explanation. (So, in the course of the experiment, each child encountered each large-set problem three times—once during the pretest, and twice during training sessions.) In training sessions, all children were told whether their answer was correct or not, and if it was not correct, they were told the correct answer

Table 5.3 Types of problems presented in Siegler's number conservation study

Problem type	Initial configuration	Operation	Final configuration
Equal	○ ○ ○ ○ ● ● ● ●	Back and forth	○ ○ ○ ○ ● ● ● ●
Length	○ ○ ○ ○ ● ● ● ●	Add or subtract	○ ○ ○ ○ ○ ● ● ● ●
Density	○ ○ ○ ○ ● ● ● ●	Add or subtract	○ ○ ○ ● ● ● ●
Conflct-length	○ ○ ○ ○ ● ● ● ●	Add or subtract	○○○ ● ● ● ●
Conflct-density	○ ○ ○ ○ ● ● ● ●	Add or subtract	○○○○○ ● ● ● ●
Conflct-equal	○ ○ ○ ○ ● ● ● ●	Lengthen or shorten	○ ○ ○ ○ ● ● ● ●

(e.g., "That's right. That row does have more," or "No, actually they have the same number of buttons.")

In addition to being told the correct answer, some children were also prompted to think about the *reasoning behind* the answer. For example, if they were correct, they were asked, "How did you know that?" If they were incorrect and were therefore told the answer, they were asked, "How do you think *I* knew that?" During each session, the experimenter recorded whether children's responses were correct, explanation(s) they gave, whether they gave one or more explanations, and whether they accurately depicted the situation. Types of explanations are listed in Table 5.4.

It is important to note that the explanations reflect different strategies that children used, and that some of these strategies are more successful than others. For example, the "length" explanation type suggests that the child is basing his decision on the *length* of the row. Children will be correct if they use it on the "length" and "conflict length" problems described in Table 5.3, but not on the other four types of problems. The "transformational" and the "counting" explanation types reflect strategies that work in *all* conditions (at least in this experiment).

Findings from this study quickly revealed that individual children, and the group as a whole, used a variety of explanations at all points in the experiment. Thus, even on tasks that are based on logical principles such as these number conservation tasks, children displayed older ways of thinking at the same time as they displayed newer ways for several sessions. These results provide more evidence that thinking is variable and the path of change is not always linear.

At a deeper level, analyses revealed something even more striking: the greater the number of distinct types of explanations children used

Table 5.4 Types of explanations children gave in Siegler's number conservation study

Explanation Type	Example
Transformational	You added one to that row, so it has more.
Length	That row is longer.
Counting	I counted, and that row has 7 and that one has 6.
Back and forth	It doesn't matter, because you put them back where they started.
Don't know	I don't know why they're the same.

on the pretest, the higher their percent correct in the training sessions. In other words, using multiple strategies, both between and within trials, was positively related to learning.

In explaining this finding, Siegler says that using varied approaches helps children learn because it provides them with empirical evidence about which approaches work best and which do not. For example, if they use a "transformational" and a "length" strategy, they may realize that the "length" strategy does not work every time, but that the transformational strategy does. In some cases, working with multiple strategies can also lead to cognitive conflict, which in turn makes children aware of possibilities and become more open to new ways of thinking. For example, if they use both a "length" and a "counting" strategy in the same trial, they may find that even though one row is longer, they reach the same number when they use the counting strategy. If they use both the "length" and the "transformational" strategies in the same trial, they may realize that the two strategies give them different answers, and they must then figure out which one is correct.

Siegler further explains that students who use a greater variety of strategies for solving problems tend to learn better subsequently. This is in part because the greater variability leads the students to be able to cope with whatever kinds of problems they encounter, rather than just being able to cope with a narrow range. In fact, about applying this idea in early childhood, Siegler explains

> high variability may benefit [children's] learning by leading to their trying many alternatives and learning how well each works. Infancy and early childhood seems a particularly appropriate time for high variability, because there is so much to learn and because the costs of non-optimal performance are not that great.

By using multiple strategies, children begin to learn important aspects of different problem situations and strategies themselves—including what information is important, which strategies take longer, and which are more often accurate.

Teacher Responses
  ◆ *This makes a lot of sense to me. If you have multiple ways to solve a problem—or you know there are multiple ways a problem can be*

solved—you are more persistent, which often leads to better problem solving. It's about building a tool box.

◆ *This helps me understand the value in having students explain their thinking out loud—around different strategies—and having students show and explain how they solved a problem. It also makes me reflect on how I need to have a balance of problems that promote the use of different strategies.*

◆ *While I had previously valued the use of multiple strategies for children, believing it leads to greater fluidity and flexibility in problem-solving, I had not truly considered how the use of multiple strategies in itself can lead to greater learning. I had previously viewed its benefit only as a necessity for building flexibility and showing greater skill with more advanced math. I had not considered that, instead, the use of multiple strategies could lead the learning.*

Conclusion

Robert Siegler's research sheds light on important aspects of children's mathematical thinking and learning. Specifically, his work has revealed that children's strategy use and the path of their learning is much more variable than previously thought—that thinking and learning do not follow linear paths—and that children who show greater variability in their thinking often learn more. His microgenetic approach to studying learning shifts the focus from learning what a student can do on one trial to what a student can learn when working on similar problems over time. The information gleaned from this approach offers insight on the way children process information and adapt ideas and strategies. This emphasis on how children's thinking changes over time can lead to important ideas related to the number and kinds of opportunities teachers provide for children's learning.

Teachers Respond to the Research

In reaction to this research, many teachers in our seminar group said that the findings resonated with their experiences in the classroom. Teachers said they see individual children using different strategies on similar problem types, and that even with small groups of children, variability in thinking and strategy use can be seen. The teachers were very interested in exploring ways that this research could inform important, practical issues related to math curriculum and instruction. Many were also provoked to think more deeply about when and how to assess student thinking. In the section below, we detail these reactions and questions, and include Bob Siegler's responses.

Features of Problems and Implications for Instruction

Teachers were interested in specific features of problems and problem types that seemed to be easier or harder for children to solve, and wanted to understand what makes them that way.

- *Reading this work, I find myself wondering why "doubles" problems, like 2 + 2, 3 + 3, and 4 + 4, are easier for children.*

- *In my experience, children often find 1 + 5 harder to solve than 5 + 1. It makes sense when you realize that "and 1 more makes ___" is something kids hear us say often. "Plus 1" addition like this is common, but starting with 1 and adding 5—or any other number— just isn't that common.*

- *I find it's important to be aware of how much information children need to keep track of in order to do a problem. And sometimes that information is just not easy to represent or remember, so kind of like the non-fives and the non-doubles, they require a bit more work across the fingers.*

This type of analysis brought teachers to an important question regarding curriculum and instruction: **Why are some problems, like "doubles," so much easier for children, and what can we learn from this research about when and how to sequence, present, and talk about problems with specific features and cognitive challenges, so that we're growing the number and types of strategies all children are experiencing?**

Siegler's Response

Siegler agreed with teachers' assessments about doubles, and explained:

Doubles are easier than other problems for at least two reasons. One reason is that parents and textbooks present them more often than other problems, giving children more opportunities to learn answers to them. The other reason is that such problems are distinctive and therefore easier to remember and associate with answers.

He also noted that the teachers are correct about "plus one" problems: he did a study that found they are more common than "one plus" problems, both in terms of what parents present and what appears in textbooks (see Siegler & Shrager, 1984). It's also true, as the teacher's comment above suggests, that "plus one" alludes to the count system in a powerful way. That is, if children know the pattern of the counting words, once they learn that "plus one" always leads to the next word in the sequence, they have a key for all such problems. To "flip" the process by mentally turning a "one plus" problem into a "plus one" (as adults commonly do) is a more sophisticated strategy and requires a working understanding of commutativity (when changing the order of the addends will not change the result).

As far as addressing the broader question about when and how to present problems, Siegler stressed beginning by thoroughly assessing what students already understand and know how to do. He also recommended providing opportunities for children to learn "alternative strategies for solving the same problem," and to have opportunities to discuss ways that the strategies differ and are related to one another. As we see elsewhere in this chapter, providing multiple strategies is a powerful technique for supporting math learning. Siegler also reminds us that "some students are more comfortable with one strategy and other students with other strategies," so providing alternatives means you are more likely to engage all students.

Time, Accuracy, and Efficiency

Related to the question above, teachers wanted to hear more about when and how they should consider issues of solution time, accuracy, and efficiency in students' strategy use and problem solving.

◆ *I think a lot of times in the classroom, there's an emphasis on doing it the quickest way. But the quickest way is not always the best way, at least for every child. We've got to value the fact that some children need to process and use longer or different strategies. As long as we're all arriving at the same answer, then that's all we should be focusing on, right?*

◆ *I am wondering what Siegler would say about trying to move children to fast and efficient strategies sooner. Can we help them? How much and what kind of help would he suggest?*

Given these kinds of concerns, we asked Siegler: **Is accuracy the best place to focus our teaching? And how does accuracy fit alongside efficiency and time it takes to solve problems?**

Siegler's Response

Siegler responded that while accuracy is the first priority, it will not ultimately be enough.

> Consider what happens if a fourth grader solves single-digit addition problems (e.g., 9 + 8) correctly 98% of the time but does so using counting strategies. Now the child has to solve multi-digit multiplication problems. If the child cannot retrieve answers to the multiplication problems quickly and accurately, counting to solve each addition will lead to the multi-digit multiplication problems taking a very long time to solve, and often to errors as well.

He also cautioned against pushing too hard for the development of new strategies in order to increase children's problem-solving speed.

> For most students, speed comes naturally, because early strategies—which tend to be slow but accurate—are increasingly replaced by strategies that are faster as well as equally or more accurate. It might seem like a paradox, but the way to increase the speed at which children get to more sophisticated strategies is to make sure that they understand and are skillful in using less sophisticated strategies. If that goal is attained, the less sophisticated strategies provide a foundation for acquiring and understanding the more sophisticated ones. For example, mastering the early strategy of counting from one makes it easier to master the later strategy of counting from the larger addend, and both make it easier to master the still later strategy of retrieving answers from memory (because students learn correct answers that they have generated earlier by counting from one or from the larger addend).

Siegler does recommend identifying and naming strategies explicitly, "so that students and teachers can discuss them with each other." By making *thinking processes* the topic of conversation, and not just *the facts*, we provide an approach, so that all children have opportunities to try out each strategy for themselves.

Understanding and Assessing Student Thinking

The teachers in our group thought deeply about the power of the microgenetic approach to understand student thinking.

> ◆ *I really value what we learn from this deep, close-up work with children over time. This approach makes me reflect on how I observe and listen to my students. I want to pay more attention to which strategies come up, when, and for whom.*

> ◆ *In my classroom, I can't focus so closely on each student because there is not enough time, but there must be ways to incorporate some of this thinking about how to understand the development of a child's thinking into my work. Suggestions?*

We asked Siegler: **What are the best ways for teachers to understand and capture information about how individual children are using strategies to solve problems? How can we help other teachers change their view that young children must discard inefficient strategies in favor of efficient strategies right away?**

Siegler's Response

As is made clear above, Siegler strongly advocates the discussion of strategies during class time as an important mechanism for learning about which children are using which strategies. To get a more fine-grained analysis, Siegler recommends using students' work to understand their strategy use over time.

> Look carefully at the homework of individual children over an entire unit—multi-digit whole number subtraction, for example, or fraction addition with equal and unequal denominators— and think about the variety of answers that the child generates on the same or highly similar problems.

Analyzing student work to understand thinking and strategy use is not easy. It takes time and practice to decipher a thought process from written evidence. However, the pay-off in terms of your understanding of both the students' mathematical ideas and the types of strategies you are likely to see is enormous. It is easier to complete this process with colleagues—different minds looking at the same piece of work will see different things. If you have colleagues teaching the same grade at your school, you can assign the same problems, and then work to analyze the results together.

Looking at student work with colleagues is also a great way to help other teachers see the value of encouraging multiple strategy use and allowing the use of "easier" strategies. One of the best ways to become aware of the problems that can arise when we push toward more sophisticated strategies is for teachers to take a deeper dive into the math content and how children are currently approaching it. When teachers analyze student work and discuss the strategies students are using, both the math and the particular child's strategy use are brought into focus in powerful ways. For some of your colleagues, this process may make clearer the need to spend more time on less sophisticated strategies as a mechanism for developing more efficient ones.

Instruction, Materials, and Multiple Strategies

Teachers were very interested in whether and how textbooks and other instructional materials align with what these research findings tell us about how students learn.

◆ *I believe strongly in meeting kids where they are, but the reality is that my math curriculum has a pacing guide, and my principal wants me to be aligned with it. Often these guides call for mastery of a strategy in a short period of time. I'm not sure how to marry these issues.*

◆ *After reading about the Overlapping Waves Model as it relates to strategy use, we can see that learning does not happen in a linear fashion, at least in the short term. But all we have to work with are materials that present strategies in a mostly linear way. I find I am often jumping around in my curriculum because of a sense of what my students need, and I think this model of strategy use supports that.*

◆ *These findings add to my concern about some of the assessment tools and standardized tests we use. It's bad enough that a snapshot of a single point in time is used to make lots of important decisions, but even more, these tools focus on end results, not strategies. That's frustrating.*

About these ideas, they asked: **Does the structure of lessons, units, and content in these materials make sense given this research? Should curriculum developers build lessons and content in some other way, based on the Overlapping Waves Model of change and strategy use?** They also wondered, **What impact could this research have on current assessment tools and standardized tests?**

Siegler's Response

Textbooks and standards such as the Common Core are starting to describe different strategies that could be used to solve problems, to encourage children to use multiple strategies, and to discuss their strengths and weaknesses. I wish they did this to a greater degree than they do, but it is starting to happen.

Assessing the strategies that children use to solve problems, as well as whether their answers are correct, might improve assessment accuracy. This has been discussed, but as far as I know, hasn't been implemented much. Assessing strategy use and providing feedback on it might encourage children to try harder to understand why different strategies work and why they're most useful in different situations.

Teachers' Ideas for Classroom Practice

Teachers in our group had several ideas about how to incorporate this research into their classroom practice. We present some of those ideas below.

Make a Habit of Observing Children Up Close, Asking Students to Explain Their Mathematical Thinking, and Listening Carefully

◆ *I mostly collect information about student thinking informally but purposefully. I take anecdotal notes about strategies students are trying after engaging in a small group activity with other students. I also make notes about mathematical thinking while observing students playing, such as dumping and filling containers at the sensory table or building with unit blocks. I spend a lot of my time asking students to explain their thinking in different ways. I ask questions such as, "How did you know that?" or "What did you do to figure that out?"*

◆ *You need to observe children in action over a period of time. You are not going to learn about how students think and learn in just one class period. Repeated, periodic observations (as are often done in preschool) should be done in all grades as a type of formative assessment used to plan your instruction.*

◆ *Engage in powerful interactions with the children in which you ask questions and provide feedback to push their thinking. It's about being in the moment with a student or small group of students, being attentive to what they are doing and asking the right questions.*

Teachers can address important findings about the complexities of children's strategy use by slowing down, looking closely, and being an active listener. Even though early childhood classrooms are busy, lively places, and time and space to pay close attention is sometimes hard to find, there are ways to develop and incorporate these valuable practices.

One way is to plan ahead to observe and interact during specific times—like "center time," for example. Or, select specific activities where you might see or hear math thinking. Start by watching and listening carefully, and then ask open-ended questions, such as "Why did you do that?"; "How did you know to look there?"; "Can you tell/show me . . .?"; or "What if . . .?" It can also be helpful to restate what you think the child is telling you, so that she can hear you making statements and has an opportunity to offer corrections or further details.

Tracking thinking over time is truly a challenge, since it requires some kind of record keeping. If there is already an observation-based assessment being used in your setting, try focusing your observations on those behaviors that really illuminate children's thinking and strategies, such as finger or manipulative use. Rather than only recording a child's accomplishment (e.g., getting the right answer), ask yourself, "What is the thinking behind this accomplishment?" In many situations it is necessary to probe for more information, such as by asking, "How did you know that?" or "How did you figure that out?" By asking these questions you might expand on a note that a child "recognized five dots on a dot card," to include the fact that she said she "knew it 'cuz it looks like that on dice."

If there is no required observation-based assessment in your setting, there are two options for tracking changes in thinking over time: 1) construct and implement such a system yourself; or 2) use ongoing student work to provide a record of strategy change. If you have to construct your own system, you can start with something simple. For example, as you move around the room during choice time, consider using a clipboard to record the date, a child's name, and details about what you see and hear that's mathematical. Pretend you're a detective! Jot down information about how students approach and solve problems. Then, examine that information for what can be learned about the student's thinking. Here is one such series of records: "On Tuesday Reyna tried to put the medium stacking cup into the small cup, which didn't work, and then successfully switched it." "On Thursday Reyna compared the medium stacking cup to the large one before putting it inside with no problems." Through regular, close-up observations like these, a teacher could see Reyna using one strategy (trial and error) and later a new, more sophisticated one (making a comparison before taking a subsequent action).

As mentioned in the *Teachers Respond to the Research* section on teachers' responses to the research, artifacts of the work that students complete during their experiences in class can provide a deep and thought-provoking record of changes in thinking. When older children begin to use labeled drawings and symbols to support their problem-seeing and solving, the related artifacts they produce can tell us a lot about the thought processes they use. What, for example, do they do to solve this problem: "Micah had five oranges, and Tanya gave him three more. How many oranges does Micah have now?" Do they draw five oranges, draw an additional three oranges, and then write the numbers one through eight below them? Do they draw a set of five oranges, a set of three oranges, and then another, "combined set" of eight oranges (so that there are a total of 16 oranges on the page) with lines connecting each one to an orange in one of the original sets? Or do they write "$5 + 3 = 8$?" Such differences tell us a lot about at least one of the strategies a child is employing.

Of course, the student work generated in kindergarten and beyond is often more easily preserved than that in preschool. Because many artifacts of preschool students' "work" are made out of reusable materials, such as blocks, baby dolls, and beads, we cannot as easily sit down and examine them in a quiet moment. For such classrooms, collecting photos, observation notes, and dictations is a better way to capture the "work." The trick is remembering to spend time creating these representations during a busy day. Fortunately, such efforts to document what is occurring can serve more than one purpose: a photo that helps you remember the new kind of bridge Samantha built can also find a home on a classroom wall, where she can look at it to remind herself what she did yesterday, and perhaps choose to improve on it!

Provide Opportunities for Young Children to See, Hear, and Try Multiple Strategies

◆ *During number talks, I ask students to explain to us how they solved a problem. If it is a new strategy to the class, we name it and write it up on the board with an example. Students can refer to this during math talks or small groups when I ask them to identify their strategy and explain their thinking.*

◆ *With preschoolers, I love to do finger play activities, like "show me four." One child will put up four fingers on one hand, and another will do two fingers on each hand. Then we talk about the different ways they both "solved the problem."*

◆ *I work with small groups of students on various types of math problems to see what their "go to" strategy is. Then I mix up students and see if they pick up on the strategies of others without it being explicitly taught.*

The key to encouraging the use of multiple strategies is to present problems that can be solved in multiple ways, to give children time to figure them out, and then to encourage discussion about the different approaches children took. This is the crux of "Number Talks" mentioned by teachers in this and several other chapters in this volume. Further, having children who have explained a new strategy *name* it (e.g., "Matthew's strategy" or "the 'make 10' strategy") gives them a voice and ownership in the process. In subsequent conversations about math, referring back to those strategies by name, and encouraging children to do so as well, will make them easier to remember and use.

More often than not, there is little need for a teacher to model a new strategy in a classroom where students are discussing their thinking, because a student will offer the strategy first. By encouraging students to show and explain their thinking, teachers include more experiences and ideas in the discussion, and thus more sophisticated strategies are likely to appear. The teacher's job is to notice what is new about a strategy, and probe the student to explain why they used it.

Of course, the process will be a little different for preschoolers: we can't ask of them what we ask of second graders, who might write or draw to explain their strategies. But we *can* set up the expectation that preschoolers will "show their thinking," even if they cannot always articulate it in words. One way to help them demonstrate their ideas is by encouraging them to use visuals, like fingers (as in the teacher's example above of having children showing four in different ways), or manipulatives. For example, when they identify how many spaces have been filled within a 10 frame, they can follow that up by telling others how they "saw it," as in, "I knew the full row on the bottom was five, and one more makes six because it's 'five, six.'" Helping children share and explain their thought processes in a way that is connected to visual representations makes math thinking visible for *all children*.

Working to make thinking visible is incredibly powerful for students, as well as for teachers. When a class works on a problem and then only discusses the *answer*, the thinking behind it is mysteriously absent: children either understand how the answer might have been derived and have their own way of finding it confirmed (*if* they were one of the students who was correct), or they know only that their method did not work, don't know why, and have no information about a more successful problem-solving strategy. Further, opportunities to increase fluency and demonstrate the value of flexible math thinking are lost when a class does not share and talk about different approaches. The process helps a child think through and clarify ideas. It solidifies strategies, so they can be described, inscribed, compared, and altered. It also helps prepare those strategies to be more readily brought to bear in new situations.

Whole group discussions are not the only way to encourage the use of multiple strategies. Partner and small-group work in which children tell one another how they approached a problem can be extremely useful. For children who are unsure about the math, unsure about using English, or shy, this provides an opportunity to speak, listen, and clarify thinking in less public settings. For older children, journaling about problem solving can help generalize approaches, though their first efforts at representing their thinking in their own journal may have to be structured and supported. You can also incorporate the use of individual whiteboards or similar tools for drawing and representing during whole group math discussion. When children "show their thinking" on these boards and hold them up at the same time (just like when preschoolers use their fingers to show "four"), those different models become a visible collection of different strategies for the same problem.

Deepen Your Own Knowledge of Problem Types and Related Strategies

◆ *This chapter makes me realize that I need to have a balance of problems that make good use of different strategies. Without the right problems, students will have no real need to try and apply them.*

◆ *I think it would be really helpful to talk with other preschool teachers about what strategies they see and teach in their classrooms. I recognize that different strategies are showing up or being used, but I don't often name them or think about how they are developing.*

It's amazing how quickly teachers' knowledge about math content deepens when they begin to focus on students' solution strategies. This kind of understanding about the math—the different ways it can be approached, the pitfalls of certain strategies, the types of situations that are more open-ended—is at the heart of what makes a great math teacher. Having knowledge about types of problems and various approaches to solving them gives teachers a real advantage for planning instruction and helping their students.

Unfortunately, many teachers feel under-prepared to select problems that will elicit certain strategies. Even when teachers are working with well-designed, developmentally appropriate instructional materials, they might reasonably worry that they will miss teachable moments if they are not prepared to handle questions on the fly or seize a meaningful learning opportunity that arises unexpectedly.

Pattern blocks, for example, are a rich and useful math resource, but many teachers have not been well-trained in how to use them and are unaware of how they provide important connections across topics in early math. The key to pattern blocks is that the small, green, equilateral triangle block can be used in multiples to replace almost all of the other, larger shapes (with two exceptions). That is, a pattern block hexagon can be made with six triangles, and a pattern block trapezoid can be made with three. This means that a pattern block puzzle that is completely filled in with a hexagon and a trapezoid could also be completed with a hexagon and three triangles, or nine triangles, or a trapezoid and six triangles. Together, these alternative strategies for achieving a similar result provide a powerful experience of equivalence achieved by composing and decomposing shapes in precise ways. If, however, a teacher does not suggest that there might be "another way" to complete a pattern block puzzle, a child might have no reason to "do it again" and these mathematical relationships between the blocks might not emerge—a missed opportunity for thinking about combining and separating, and what it means to be "the same."

Recall that rather than explicitly introducing a strategy to the class, the best practice is to allow it to emerge organically through problem solving and group discussions. If you are aware of a strategy that is not arising, look at the problems you are presenting: eliciting a new strategy might require a new type of problem situation. For example, if you want children to figure out the strategy of flipping over shapes in order to change their presentation, provide shapes that do not have a line of symmetry (e.g., the parallelogram in a tangram set), and create a problem situation that requires the shape to be flipped (e.g., Figure 5.3). Taken together, teacher knowledge and instructional choices, along with student knowledge and problem-solving choices, deepen and expand everyone's opportunity to learn and do mathematics.

There are many resources teachers can use to learn more about problem and strategy types. Convening a small group of colleagues and studying such resources is often the best way to learn. By focusing on one topic, tool, or solution approach, such as cardinal number

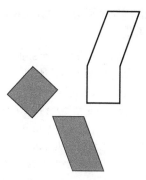

Figure 5.3 Problem selected to encourage "flipping" as a strategy to transform a shape

sense, pattern blocks, or "plus one" strategies, you can focus in depth, taking time to read, discuss, try new problem types in your classroom, and review your results with colleagues. For example, using Sherry Parrish's *Number Talks* (Parrish, 2010), you might focus on problems that help develop fluency up to five, and use example exercises she provides that employ different tools, trying "dot cards" one week, and using "5-frames" the next. By documenting student results and analyzing them with other teachers, your knowledge of relationships between children's cardinal understanding of small numbers and the types of problems that foster it will increase substantially. We include a list of books at the end of this chapter that we have found work well for this kind of study.

Even without using a teaching resource, studying student work can similarly increase teacher knowledge about problem types and related strategies. In order to understand what children's artifacts indicate about strategy use, teachers must look deeply, imagining the thought processes behind the written or drawn work. When student work is compared and thoughtfully analyzed, what are at first subtle differences in their representations quickly become clues to different choices and levels of understanding. By working with teachers from other classrooms, and analyzing the work of not only your own, but also their students, it may become clear that certain strategies are appearing in one classroom but not another. This, in turn, can prompt thinking about which math problems and provocations might be used as productive next steps. Again, through engaging closely with information from students and attempting to understand it, your knowledge about approaches to problem-solving and types of problems will expand.

Consider Early Childhood a Time When Variability in Thinking Can Really Pay Off!

◆ *In my classroom, I see that the more specific my lessons get around which strategy a child should use, the less students are engaged across the board, whether they "get it" immediately or not. It's as if what I'm asking is for them to simply check a box and if they check it they are done. If they don't know how to do this, then they accept that they can't do it. I think my lessons that are more context-based and ask the students to solve problems in their own way not only lead to more understanding in different ways but more engagement.*

◆ *I think an important idea I've read about here is related to the word "cope." We want students who fail in getting a correct answer to keep trying and to have other strategies and ways to move forward rather than just feeling like they've already used the only idea they knew to help them.*

Meaningful and generative learning experiences in school usually happen as a result of productive struggle and failed attempts. And productive struggle can only occur when children feel safe to ask questions and are supported and encouraged to try again, or to explore new ideas. If a teaching goal is to help children learn how to learn in general, it makes sense to work to enhance curiosity, increase exposure to diverse ways of thinking, and seek meaningful opportunities in which children can apply what they are learning. During a child's years in school, mistakes should not be terribly consequential. Obvious as it seems, sometimes it's useful to remind ourselves that the goal is not right answers, but student learning and growth—this lesson is especially important in mathematics, which many mistakenly see as "cut and dried."

And if this is true of school in general, then how much more relevant is it during the early childhood portion of that schooling? Siegler's work indicates that between 3 and 8 years of age is a particularly important time to experiment with multiple approaches. In many cultures, humans believe this is a period when children should be protected and cared for—nurtured instead of having to nurture others—and expected to focus on their own development. This belief about the importance of experiences and opportunities as opposed to accomplishments has pervaded preschool education for many years. Previously, it was a value that strongly influenced the kindergarten and early elementary school years as well, but with standardized assessments looming in the third grade year, most US schools now offer a more pressured version of learning for five, six, and seven year olds. Given what we know from Siegler's work, it seems logical that preserving a sense of play and possibility will not only make school and math more enjoyable; it will also enable children to learn math meaningfully and flexibly. If we can avoid the "one right way" message that has dominated mathematics teaching and learning for many years, and instead foster and preserve a sense of exploration and creativity, we will be contributing to a much-needed shift in math education.

The Bottom Line

Siegler's microgenetic approach to cognitive developmental research shows us that young children often know and can use several strategies at one time, rather than moving from one approach to another in a step-by-step fashion. This is true even when one strategy is more efficient than another: both may be maintained for quite some time. It is also clear that having and using more strategies at any given point is beneficial to learning, both in the moment and in the future. That is, the more strategies a child has for solving similar problems, the more they are likely to learn and be able to do. Finally, the number of strategies a child has available to her or him can change; children can learn strategies through seeing them work, talking about them with others, and trying them themselves.

To provide young children with excellent early math learning experiences, it is important for teachers to recognize and encourage many different types of problem-solving strategies. Teachers can do this by focusing the class's attention on strategies, discussing and comparing them. Incorporating multiple ways of modeling and representing math thinking into teaching can help students learn to share their approaches and recognize new approaches that others are using. It's also useful to pay close attention to what strategies children are and are not using, as this can guide choices about what kinds of contexts and problems the teacher should focus on next.

Teacher Resources

Carpenter, T. P. (Eds.) (©1999) *Children's mathematics: Cognitively guided instruction*. Portsmouth, NH: Heinemann.

Clements, D. H., and Sarama, J. (2009). *Learning and teaching early math: The learning trajectories approach*. New York: Routledge.

Early Math Collaborative—Erikson Institute. (2014). *Big ideas of early mathematics: What teachers of young children need to know*. New York: Pearson.

Parrish, S. (2010). *Number talks: Helping children build mental math and computation strategies*. Sausalito, CA: Math Solutions.

Shumway, J. F. (2010). *Number sense routines: Building numerical literacy every day in Grades K-3*. Portland, ME: Stenhouse.

Selected References

Siegler, R. S. (1995). How does change occur: A microgenetic study of number conservation. *Cognitive Psychology, 28,* 225–273.

Siegler, R. S. (1996). *Emerging minds: The process of change in children's thinking.* New York: Oxford University Press.

Siegler, R. S. (2005). Children's learning. *American Psychologist, 60,* 769–778.

Siegler, R. S. (2007). Cognitive variability. *Developmental Science, 10,* 104–109.

Siegler, R. S., and Jenkins, E. (1989). *How children discover new strategies.* Hillsdale, NJ: Lawrence Erlbaum Associates, Inc.

Siegler, R. S., and Robinson, M. (1982). The development of numerical understandings. In H. W. Reese and L. P. Lipsitt (Eds.), *Advances in child development and behavior,* p. 16. New York: Academic Press.

Siegler, R. S., and Shrager, J. (1984). Strategy choices in addition and subtraction: How do children know what to do? In C. Snow (Ed.), *Origins of Cognitive skills,* pp. 229–292. Hillsdale, NJ: Lawrence Erlbaum Associates, Inc.

6

Pathways to Basic Combination Fluency in the Primary Grades

Jeanine O'Nan Brownell and Mary Hynes-Berry, with Arthur J. Baroody

Many people believe that single-digit addition and subtraction facts such as 2 + 2 = 4 and 4 − 3 = 1 must be memorized by rote and that drill (solving problems repeatedly and receiving feedback on correctness) is the best means for achieving this goal. Yet, over the last five decades, there have been major advances in what we know about children's mathematical learning in general and the best ways to help children learn the basic number combinations in particular.

Arthur J. Baroody, Professor Emeritus at the University of Illinois, is an educational and developmental psychologist who has spent almost 40 years investigating how children *do* learn the number facts, or what he prefers to call number *combinations*, because "facts" connote unrelated information that must each be learned and stored in memory separately. We talked with him about how his own beliefs have shifted over time as a result of studying children's informal strategies for figuring out sums and differences. Baroody has contributed to our understanding of what it means to "memorize" these number combinations, and his work has helped expand the definition of *fluency* with such combinations (see Concept Box 6.1). His research has more recently focused on the role of adult guidance in developing basic fact fluency—a topic with many implications for teachers and parents alike.

Concept Box 6.1   Fluency

Fluency with basic facts has traditionally meant fast and accurate recall. In recent decades, the definition of fact fluency has been expanded to include the **flexible** and **appropriate**, as well as the **efficient** and **accurate**, production of arithmetic combinations using reasoning strategies, as well as fact recall (National Research Council, 2009). Baroody argues that when instruction focuses on memorizing basic facts by rote, many—but not all—children can achieve efficient and accurate fact recall or "partial fluency." That is, such children often can't apply their factual knowledge flexibly and appropriately to new problems or contexts. In contrast, when instruction focuses on meaningful memorization (i.e., recognizing and using patterns and relationships), children can achieve "true fluency." In other words, they can thoughtfully (flexibly and appropriately) as well as quickly and accurately use their knowledge of number combinations to solve new problems. For example, children with "true fluency" of the facts $5 + 5 = 10$ and $5 + 1 = 6$ not only can retrieve those combinations quickly and accurately, but they also can also use them to logically figure out the sum of an unknown combination, such as $6 + 5$: As 6 is one more than 5 and the sum of $5 + 5$ is 10, the sum of $5 + 6$ must be one more than 10 or 11.

Teacher Responses
◆ *This expanded definition of "fluency" means that fluency really is the Holy Grail. If you have this, you have access to mathematical thinking and problem solving. You see relationships. You know it conceptually. You can access it even if you forget it. You built it.*

What the Research Says

Conventional wisdom suggests that if you want a child to know $2 + 3 = 5$, you tell the child this number fact and then you have him or her practice it until it's automatic. The rationale for "drilling" children is that people learn by association: you have $2 + 3$ and you have 5, and you have to form a connection between the two. The more often people hear "$2 + 3$" and "5" together, the more likely they are to make an association and then be able to automatically say the correct answer when asked the sum of $2 + 3$. This rationale reflects a behaviorist theory of learning. **Behaviorism** holds that learning is the result of conditioning the learner to a set of habits—in this case, the ability to find basic sums and differences. In this view, children are, in effect, programmed to produce the right answers.

As an undergraduate education major at Cornell in the 1960s, Baroody was taught behaviorism, the dominant theory of learning at the time. Returning to Cornell in the 1970s as a graduate student, though, he encountered a different perspective of learning, **constructivism**, which was built on the theories of Jean Piaget. In a course taught by the developmental psychologist Herbert Ginsburg, Baroody learned that children are not simply passive learners (empty vessels that need to be filled with knowledge) but active thinkers and constructors of knowledge. In this view, the learner selects and transforms information, develops hypotheses, and generates new ideas.

Baroody recalls one reading from Ginsburg's course that was particularly influential in revolutionizing his views about how the basic combinations are learned and should be taught. In the chapter, William A. Brownell (1935), who was reacting to the popular (behaviorist) drill approach, proposed a "meaning" theory. In his view, arithmetic should be conceived of as "a closely knit system of understandable ideas, principles, and processes." For Brownell, the true test of learning was "not mere mechanical facility in 'figuring'" but an intelligent grasp and application of number relations. Whereas proponents of drill theory viewed children's informal counting and reasoning strategies as immature methods or even as crutches that interfered with the real effort of memorizing basic facts by rote, Brownell viewed such informal strategies as crucial—when children determine sums and differences in a way that makes sense to them, it leads to the *meaningful* memorization of the basic combinations.

Baroody said that he was intrigued by the idea that the basic combinations—like other worthwhile knowledge—embodied numerous patterns and relations, and that learning this body of knowledge was an active, rather than a passive, process. It was fascinating to him that young children, without explicit instruction, could make sense of arithmetic situations and devise their own counting and reasoning strategies for determining sums and differences. He found compelling the idea that children's memory of basic combinations might embody patterns and relations they had discovered. This would indicate that children could have more meaningful pathways to learning basic combinations than memorizing by rote numerous, separate facts.

Inventing Counting Strategies to Solve Addition Problems

Although Baroody had learned about constructivism from Ginsburg, a series of experiences fully convinced him of the validity of this view. Early in his career, Baroody worked one-on-one with kindergartners, and the aim was to document how children's ability to determine sums developed over time.

In a 1987 study, each child was interviewed 13 times over the course of 8 months. In each session, Baroody presented the children with a set of 10 cards on which a horizontal addition problem was typed (e.g., 2 + 3). The problems varied in difficulty, with addends ranging from 1 to 7 and sums ranging from 4 to 10. Baroody also read the problem aloud, saying, for example, "This says 2 and 3. How much are 2 and 3 altogether?" He invited children to solve the problem any way they wanted—using fingers or blocks, or doing it mentally. All problems were given with the smaller addend first (e.g., 2 + 5 instead of 5 + 2) to see if children would figure out that starting with the larger addend, even if it is second, produces the same answer and is faster.

Baroody recorded and categorized the specific ways that the children solved the problems, including how they represented the addends, whether they counted them or not, and how they figured out the sums. One purpose of the frequent interviews was to catch children in the process of constructing new counting strategies to find sums. The children received little formal math instruction during their half-day kindergarten program, so the interviews constituted the bulk of their addition experience (at least in the school setting).

A main distinction that Baroody made in his observations of children was whether they used *concrete* or *abstract* counting strategies to find the sums. When children are first learning to add, they use concrete counting strategies. This type of strategy involves two separate processes: one to represent the addends, and one to determine the sum. So, for 3 + 5, a child might count out three fingers on one hand ("1, 2, 3") to represent the first addend, count out five fingers on the other hand ("1, 2, 3, 4, 5") to represent the second addend, and then count all of the fingers raised to determine the sum ("1, 2, 3, 4, 5, 6, 7, 8"). Baroody recorded 18 different types of concrete strategies, many of which involved *shortcuts* that the children developed in order to make the process faster.

Eventually, without being explicitly taught them, children adopt *abstract* counting strategies. This means that they use their fingers to simultaneously represent the addends *and* determine the sum. They do this by employing a mental **keeping-track process** that tells them when to stop counting. For example, for 3 + 5, a child might start with 3 on one hand and count "1, 2, 3." Then, while raising more fingers one at a time, the child counts, "4 [is *one* more], 5 [is *two* more], 6 [is *three* more], 7 [is *four* more], 8 [is *five* more]." (Note that the words in brackets signify how the child is mentally keeping track of how many more than three he has counted.) Children who adopt these strategies realize (if only implicitly) that they do not need to count the addends separately and ahead of time like they do in the concrete counting strategies: they can arrive at the same answer in a faster way.

Baroody found that most children started the study already knowing a concrete strategy or able to learn one within a few sessions. However, he found important differences among kindergartners' readiness to learn and use more advanced strategies. He was surprised that many children—10 out of 17—never adopted abstract strategies over the course of the study, even if they started the study knowing how to use concrete counting strategies. His conclusion was that we should expect many, or even most, preschool and even kindergarten children to rely on concrete counting strategies for a long time. As he had noted in Brownell's writing, children need to use these methods in order to build an understanding of how numbers combine to make new numbers.

Baroody did observe that seven children in his study used abstract counting strategies: one started the study already using abstract counting strategies, and the rest adopted them over the course of the 13 sessions. He identified four types of abstract counting strategies, described in Table 6.1 below. These are categorized in two ways. The first is where the children start the counting process: at the number 1 ("counting all") or the cardinal value of one of the addends ("counting on"). The second is whether children start counting with the first addend or the larger addend (recall that in all problems the larger addend was given second).

Baroody was particularly interested in the order in which children developed different abstract counting strategies. He wanted to understand how children make a key transition between the most basic abstract strategy, *counting-all starting from the first* addend (Strategy A) and the most advanced and efficient counting strategy of all—*counting-on from the larger* addend (Strategy D). For 3 + 5, the former would involve starting with three fingers raised on one hand and counting "1, 2, 3," and then, while raising five more fingers, counting, "4 [is *one* more], 5 [is *two* more], 6 [is *three* more], 7 [is *four* more], 8 [is *five* more]." The latter involves starting the count with the cardinal value of the larger addend: "5," and then, while raising three more fingers,

Table 6.1 Abstract counting strategies using 3 + 5 as an example

	Start at first addend	Start at second (larger) addend
Start counting process at "1" (count all)	**Strategy A. Counting-all starting with the first addend:** "1, 2, 3... 4 [is 1 more], 5 [is 2 more], 6 [is 3 more], 7 [is 4 more], 8 [is 5 more]"	**Strategy B. Counting-all starting with the larger addend:** "1, 2, 3, 4, 5... 6 [is 1 more], 7 [is 2 more], 8 [is 3 more]"
Start counting process at cardinal value of an addend ("count on")	**Strategy C. Counting-on from the first addend:** "3... 4 [is 1 more], 5 [is 2 more], 6 [is 3 more], 7 [is 4 more], 8 [is 5 more]"	**Strategy D. Counting-on from the larger addend:** "5... 6 [is 1 more], 7 [is 2 more], 8 [is 3 more]"

Note: The count for the keeping-track process (the portions above in brackets: [is 1 more, is 2 more. . .]) is executed at the same time as the sum count (the portions not in brackets). A keeping-track count may be mental, as shown in this table, done by successively raising fingers until a child senses the correct number of fingers have been raised, or by verbally counting the fingers as they are raised counting, "6 *[is one more]*, 7 *[is two more]*, 8 *[is three more]*." Note that Strategy D entails two shortcuts: (a) starting with cardinal number 5 (instead of counting from 1 to 5) and (b) starting with larger addend, 5 (instead of the first addend, 3).

At the time, it was commonly believed that children must adopt the strategy of counting-**on** from the **first** addend (Strategy C) before getting to Strategy D. In other words, children must figure out that they can "count on" from the cardinal value of the first addend before they discover that the order of the addends does not matter. However, Baroody discovered that children commonly invented a strategy not previously reported in the research literature: counting-**all** starting with the **larger** addend (Strategy B). Furthermore, this strategy was the more common transition to Strategy D.

To this day, he remembers the kindergartner, Felicia, whom he first saw use this strategy a few years earlier. He recounted the following when we talked:

> *Well, Felicia surprised me by doing this—for 3 + 5 she counted: "1, 2, 3, 4, 5, 6 [is one more], 7 [is two more], 8 [is three more]. Felicia's strategy made a lot of sense because she had to keep track of only three counts, whereas if you start with 3, she would have had to keep track of five counts. So, for an abstract strategy, starting with the larger addend makes a lot of sense because it saves computational effort. Now, had anyone taught her this? No. This was a strategy she had devised on her own, and it's just a nice example of the power of informal thinking and strategies that kids will come up with to solve problems.*

Baroody was excited by how creative and inventive the kindergarten children he studied were. He saw firsthand how important the counting strategies were for children as they learned how to compute sums, and also how resourceful they could be in finding ways to shortcut or reduce their computational effort.

Teacher Responses
◆ *I find that most children are naturally thinking about being more efficient. I see it when children are ready, and they're like,* "I need to do this faster. This is a lot of work to count and then count and then count again." *Maybe they're just ready to be efficient*

with not only counting on but starting with the larger number, so they know they have to count less.

Beyond Counting Strategies to Basic Combination Fluency

Baroody's work and that of many others indicate that there are three phases in developing fluency with basic combinations. In **Phase 1**, children use counting to determine the sum. Computing by counting can result in the discovery of patterns and relationships that provide the basis for inventing *reasoning strategies*. Reasoning about number combinations moves children into **Phase 2** (see Table 6.2 for examples). Consider, for example, a story Baroody tells about two kindergarten girls who were playing a board game that involved throwing dot dice to determine the number of spaces a racecar could move around a track. One girl rolled a 6 and a 1 and was stumped. Her helpful playmate leaned over to her and whispered, *"That's easy, it's just the next number after six when you count."* The playmate

Table 6.2 Examples of reasoning strategies that children develop in Phase 2

Problem type	Reasoning strategy	Description
Add 1 (6 + 1, 1 + 5)	Number-after rule	For 6 + 1, think about what number comes after 6.
Doubles (3 + 3, 5 + 5)	Analogies to everyday situations, knowledge of even numbers	For 6 + 6, think about 2 rows of 6 eggs each in an egg carton. Remember that doubles always have to be even.
Addition of two addends one unit apart (3 + 4, 6 + 5)	Near doubles or doubles plus/minus one	For 5 + 6, think, "If 5 + 5 = 10, and 5 + 1 = 6, then 5 + 6 must equal one more than 10, which is 11."
Addition of two addends two units apart (3 + 5, 6 + 8)	Make a double	For 6 + 8, think "Take 1 from 8 and give it to the 6 to make 7 + 7, which is 14."
Add with 9 (5 + 9, 9 + 7)	Use 10	For 9 + 5, think, "If 10 + 5 = 15, and 9 is one less than 10, then 9 + 5 is one less than 15."
Subtraction (8-5, 9-4)	Subtraction as addition	For 8 − 5, think, "5 plus *what* equals 8?"

had noticed that, as long as you know the counting sequence, you can just say the next number in any problem that calls for adding 1, including single and multi-digit problems that they previously had not practiced (e.g., 16 + 1). The *number-after* rule, then, is an important reasoning strategy because it enables children to use what they know to logically deduce sums of unknown combinations involving the addition of 1.

Throughout Phase 2, children discover numerous patterns and relationships, such as that the sums of doubles are all even numbers. Some combinations, such as 5 + 3, can be transformed into a double by taking 1 from one addend (the 5) and giving it to the other (e.g., for 5 + 3, 1 can be taken from the 5 and given to the 3 to create 4 + 4). Knowledge of the doubles can also be used to solve addition problems in which the two addends are one unit apart using the "near doubles" strategy. For example, the known fact 5 + 5 = 10 and the number-after rule can be used to logically deduce the sum of the new combination 6 + 5: If 5 + 5 = 10, 6 is 1 more than 5, and 1 more than 10 is the number after it, then the sum of 6 + 5 must be 11.

Baroody (2016) considers the development of reasoning strategies in Phase 2 to be a critical transition from Phase 1 counting strategies to developing fluent retrieval of basic combinations (**Phase 3**). This pathway is very different from rote memorization. One reason is that discovered patterns or relationships can provide children with an organizing framework for learning and storing combinations in memory. For instance, 3 + 5 = 8 and 5 + 3 = 8 may not be stored as separate facts and recalled separately. They may instead be stored as the triad 3-5-8. A second reason is that, with practice, reasoning strategies can become automatic (efficient and non-conscious) and facilitate the fact-retrieval process. In other words, fluency may not involve fact recall exclusively but may also embody mathematical regularities (patterns and relationships). Knowledge of the triad 3-5-8, for example, could also serve to embody the relationship between addition and subtraction (e.g., 8 − 5 = 3 is related to 3 + 5 = 8). As reasoning strategies become more automatic, children retrieve facts with less and less conscious calculation.

The three phases of developing fluency summarized in Table 6.3, then, are intricately interlinked, with later phases building on earlier ones. A key implication of this model of meaningful memorization is that promoting fluency with basic combinations entails a long-term

Table 6.3 Three phases of developing fluency with the basic sums and differences (single-digit addition combinations and their complementary subtraction combinations)

Phase 1: Counting strategies—using object counting (e.g., fingers, blocks) or verbal counting to determine an answer

Phase 2: Reasoning strategies—using known information (e.g., known facts, number relationships) to logically determine the answer of an unknown combination

Phase 3: Fluent retrieval—automatic and accurate production of answers

---

process of building number sense. As suggested by William Brownell (1935), flexible, adaptive knowledge of number combinations cannot be readily drilled into children using a behaviorist approach.

> ***Teacher Responses***
> ◆ *To give children enough opportunities to discover some of these reasoning strategies on their own, it's going to be a long process. The speed will come when they truly understand it. That takes time. But time isn't what our schools allow us to have with children this age.*

The Role of Instruction in Developing Basic Combination Fluency

The decades Baroody spent conducting fieldwork with young children showed that they can and do construct new concepts and invent new strategies. At the same time, his work made it clear that many children, particularly those struggling with school mathematics, need some kind of guidance to develop certain strategies. His next goal was to determine what types of instruction might help children learn the reasoning strategies that underlie fluent retrieval of the basic combinations.

Different Approaches to Instruction

Based on his own and others' work, Baroody concluded that two approaches to teaching learning strategies tended to be unsuccessful (see Table 6.4 for a layout of different approaches). The first is *direct instruction* of the strategies, or explicitly telling children what they are. Consider the near-doubles reasoning strategy—that a combination of two addends one unit apart (e.g., 3 + 4) can be solved by adding 1 from or subtracting 1 from a known double (e.g., for 3 + 4, adding to 1 to the sum of 3 + 3 or subtracting 1 from the sum of 4 + 4). Simply telling children this strategy (and even explaining the rationale for the strategy) may not make sense to many of them and, as a result, some may misapply the strategy. For example, if the near-doubles strategy is learned without comprehension, they might mistakenly reason that 3 + 4 is 1 less than the answer to 3 + 3, arriving at the incorrect sum of 5 (Baroody, 2016).

An alternative to direct instruction is "discovery learning," in which children discover strategies on their own. Researchers have categorized discovery learning in different ways, including *unguided* and *guided* discovery. Unguided discovery involves learning through unstructured, child-chosen activities without adult feedback, such as in "free play." So, a child might incidentally become more proficient at +1 facts when playing a board game with standard dice. Research indicates, however, that unguided discovery learning is typically inefficient or even ineffective (Alfieri, Brooks, Aldrich, and Tenenbaum, 2011).

Baroody therefore looked toward guided discovery. In this approach, opportunities are created for learners to engage with specific materials that support them in constructing understanding of a targeted procedure or concept. Research shows that this is often more effective than unguided discovery or direct instruction (Alfieri et al., 2011). However, the amount of structure or guidance can vary considerably. Two categories of guided discovery that Baroody has distinguished are *highly guided discovery* and *minimally guided discovery*. Highly guided discovery involves well-structured instruction and practice that provides considerable scaffolding to direct a child's attention to regularities or a target strategy. Feedback provides some explanation of why a response is correct or incorrect. Minimally guided discovery involves less structured instruction and practice, with feedback provided on correctness only.

To investigate what kind of discovery learning is most beneficial for children, Baroody developed different computer-based interventions for kindergarten through second graders that promoted discovery of reasoning strategies in different ways. The measure of effectiveness was children's fast and accurate retrieval of practiced combinations as well as their fast, accurate, appropriate, and flexible *transfer* to unpracticed but related combinations. The latter is particularly important because it indicates that a child has learned and achieved efficient use of reasoning strategies, not merely memorized some facts by rote. In other words, *transfer* to new problems is key because it indicates adaptive (flexible and appropriate) use of a strategy, a hallmark of fluency.

Table 6.4 Different approaches to number combination/fact learning, descriptions of activities, and corresponding research findings

Broad learning theory	Fact/ combination learning theory	Approach to instruction	Research findings
Behaviorism: Children are passive learners. Learning occurs by association or by habit formation.	Children learn number "facts" by **association** (tell them "3 + 2" and "5" enough times, they will associate these with one another).	**Rote memorization of facts:** Have children memorize "facts" in isolation from one another. Tell children every number fact; then have them practice them again and again with feedback (drill) until they memorize them. Counting is regarded negatively.	Extremely inefficient (children must learn every fact (e.g., 81 sums for the numbers 1–9) separately; unpleasant & usually ineffective. At best, produces "partial fluency."
	Children learn strategies as a **habit** by being shown and then practicing them.	**Direct instruction of reasoning strategies:** Explicitly tell children what the reasoning strategies are; then have them practice using them.	Often ineffective because children may not be ready to understand them and may misapply the strategy
Constructivism: Children are active thinkers and constructors of knowledge. As they are ready, the learner selects and transforms information, develops hypotheses, and generates new ideas.	After much practice using counting strategies, children learn **reasoning strategies** to figure out number combinations based on prior knowledge. Finally, they can automatically and accurately produce answers.	**Discovery Learning:** Have children discover arithmetic regularities and use them to devise reasoning strategies on their own.	
		Unguided discovery: Unstructured activity (often "free play") with no teacher feedback	Inefficient, often ineffective—children may not discover a reasoning strategy
		Minimally guided discovery: Modestly structured instruction and practice; Feedback provided on correctness only.	Can be effective in promoting true fluency for relatively easy strategies involving relatively obvious patterns or relations (e.g., the $n + 0 = n$ rule or the **number after** rule for add-1 facts)

Highly guided discovery: Well-structured instruction and practice; Considerable scaffolding directing child's attention to regularities or a target strategy; Feedback provides some explanation of why a response is correct or incorrect.

Effective for promoting true fluency for relatively difficult strategies such as Doubles, Use-10, and Subtraction-as-Addition

Highly Guided Versus Minimally Guided Discovery Learning for Relatively Easy Problems

In several studies, Baroody and his colleagues first examined how children construct strategies to solve two relatively easy problem types: add-1 (e.g., 2 + 1; 1 + 3; 4 + 1) and doubles (e.g., 2 + 2; 3 + 3; 4 + 4). Research indicates that, aside from add-0 combinations, these are among the easiest sums for children to learn, and a likely place to first expect fluency by kindergartners or first-graders (e.g., Baroody, Purpura, Eiland, & Reid, 2015). Baroody varied the type of instruction in three training conditions: *Highly guided add-1 training*, *Highly guided doubles training*, and *Minimally guided add-1 and doubles training*.

The experimental interventions supplemented regular classroom mathematics instruction and involved two 30-minute computer sessions per week for 12 weeks. Guidance in both *highly guided* conditions involved (a) ensuring children had mastered developmental prerequisites for a strategy (e.g., knowing the counting number sequence), and (b) arranging problems sequentially to highlight a relationship and the context in which that relationship was applicable. For example, the question, *"What number comes after 3 when we count?"* was directly followed by the question, *"3 + 1 = ?,"* which was followed by the question *"1 + 3 = ?"* For doubles facts, the highly guided experience gave questions referencing everyday instances of doubling (e.g., "two rows of 6 eggs each in an egg carton is how many eggs altogether?") followed by analogous symbolic problems (e.g., "6 + 6 = ?"). Doubles training also guided children to discover that the sum of a doubles is always an even number. Children in the *minimally guided* condition practiced the same add-1 or doubles combinations as often as did participants in each of the highly guided trainings. However, the order of the items was random, not connected to prior knowledge or other conceptual knowledge, and feedback focused on correctness only.

In several respects, the results of the research confirmed expectations. First, in terms of learning the practiced doubles, both the highly and minimally guided discovery of the doubles strategy was more effective than the add-1 training, which involved no instruction or practice on the doubles. That is, practicing the doubles was more helpful than not practicing them. Second, in terms of learning the practiced add-1 combinations, both the highly and minimally guided discovery of the number-after rule strategy was more effective than the doubles training, which entailed no instruction or practice on adding 1. That is, practicing the add-1 combinations was more helpful than not practicing them. Third, for promoting transfer to *unpracticed* doubles (new doubles combinations) the highly guided discovery was more effective than both the minimally guided discovery of doubles strategies or the add-1 training.

However, Baroody was surprised to discover that the highly guided discovery intervention did not produce more learning than the minimally guided discovery intervention for add-1 facts: both guided discovery interventions were *equally* effective in promoting transfer to unpracticed add-1 facts. Baroody and his colleagues concluded that most primary-age children are so familiar with the *number-after* relations in the counting sequence that they readily see the connection between this prior knowledge and adding-1 sums: they need relatively little guidance to invent the number-after strategy. In contrast, the connections between the doubles and their everyday analogies or to even numbers are less obvious, and children seem to need more guidance to make these connections.

Highly Guided Versus Minimally Guided Discovery Learning for Relatively Difficult Problems

Next Baroody and his colleagues investigated the impact of guided discovery for learning more difficult reasoning strategies including the "use 10" strategy for add-with-8 or -9 combinations (e.g., for 9 + 5, think, "if 10 + 5 = 15, and 9 is one less than 10, then 9 + 5 is one less than 15") and the "subtraction as addition" strategy (e.g., for 8 – 5, think, "What plus 5 equals 8?"). In these reasoning strategies children use knowledge of an easier combination as well as logical thinking to deduce an unknown and difficult sum or difference.

In multiple studies (e.g., Baroody, Purpura, Eiland, Reid, & Paliwal, 2016), children worked on a computer for 30-minute sessions,

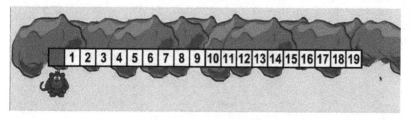

Figure 6.1 Image of "Mocha Monkey" used in Baroody's computer interventions

twice a week for 12 weeks (see Figure 6.1). Children were again randomly assigned to one of three conditions: *Highly guided use-10 training*, *Highly guided subtraction training*, and *Minimally guided use-10 and subtraction training* (see Table 6.5 for examples).

As in the previous study, both highly guided conditions arranged problems sequentially to highlight a relationship and the context in which that relationship was applicable. For example, in the "highly guided use-10" condition children solved an "add-10" item and then a related add-8 or -9 item to help them discover that the sum of the latter was 2 or 1 less than the former. In the "highly guided subtraction-as-addition" condition, items were ordered to help children discover two key ideas related to *part-whole relations*: (a) addition and subtraction are inverse operations (i.e., adding 9 can be undone by subtracting 9) and (b) there are families of combinations—addition and subtraction facts that have the same three numbers (e.g., $3 + 5 = 8$, $5 + 3 = 8$, $8 - 5 = 3$, and $8 - 3 = 5$). In the minimally guided condition children received the same amount of time on the computer and the same amount of practice with the facts as in the highly guided discovery interventions, but practiced items in no particular order, and without any connections to concepts (see Appendix for more information about how the highly-guided program worked).

When they tested the children at least 2 weeks after the intervention, the researchers found that for a given reasoning strategy, children in the two groups that received relevant training (*highly guided* for that strategy and *minimally guided* for both strategies)—while performing better than the group that only received training on the other strategy—performed *equally* to one another on practiced items. This means that for

Table 6.5 Examples of Computer Game Questions

Highly guided practice of "Use 10" strategy	Highly guided practice of "Subtraction as addition" strategy	Minimally guided practice
Mocha Monkey swings **7** branches and then **10** more, where will she land? Related add-**9** question follows: Cocoa Monkey swings **7** branches and then **9** more, where will she land?	Mocha Monkey swings **7** branches and then **9** more, where will she land? Related subtraction follows: If Mocha Monkey is at **16**, where will she be if she swings back **9**?	Mocha Monkey swings **7** branches and then **9** more, where will she land? Unrelated question follows: Cocoa Monkey starts at branch **14** and swings back **9** branches, where will she land?

practiced items, whether children received highly or minimally guided practice did not appear to matter. More importantly, the researchers found that children in the highly guided conditions performed better on *unpracticed* (new) items of the same type than either the minimally guided discovery group or the group that received the other training. In other words, while minimally guided discovery improved speed and accuracy on practiced combinations (indication of partial fluency), it did not improve speed or accuracy on related but unpracticed combinations. In contrast, highly guided discovery resulted in improved speed and accuracy with *unpracticed, as well as practiced*, combinations. This indicates that only highly guided discovery fostered learning of a reasoning strategy that could be applied flexibly and appropriately to unpracticed combinations, and therefore "true fluency."

Based on his work, Baroody argued that guided discovery learning has unique beneficial effects on promoting transfer to new problems. He also concluded that the most important factor in developing fluency may not be the *amount* but the *kind* of practice. Structured practice that promotes the discovery of mathematical relationships may play an important role in enabling children to flexibly solve new but related combinations and progress toward fluency.

Baroody also recognizes that different reasoning strategies may require different approaches. Patterns and number relationships differ in their salience to children. Less guidance seems to be needed for relationships that are more apparent to young children, such as the idea that adding zero does not change a number or the number-after rule for adding 1. In these cases, simply having children practice problems and receive feedback may work in helping children discover the reasoning strategies. On the other hand, more structured discovery learning activities may be needed for less obvious ones, such as the doubles, use-10, and subtraction-as-addition strategies.

Conclusion

Baroody spent decades studying children (including his own) and preparing early childhood teachers to teach mathematics. This gave him the opportunity to work directly with young children and teachers—to try out constructivist instructional practices (e.g., guided discovery learning) in real classrooms and evaluate first-hand their effectiveness, and to design large-scale research studies within real educational settings. Such experiences were invaluable to contributing to developmental and education theory and formulating useful and practical instructional guidelines.

Baroody argues that compelling children to memorize number facts by rote makes learning unnecessarily difficult, inefficient, and unpleasant. Ultimately, meaningful memorization of basic combinations is not only easier and more efficient; it is also more engaging and more efficacious. Further, Baroody makes a strong case that meaningful and fluent knowledge of basic combinations cannot be imposed on children. To achieve combination fluency, children need to be given the opportunity and encouragement to use counting strategies and to discover patterns and relationships. They need to be given the opportunity and encouragement to invent, apply, and (in time) automate reasoning strategies. In a real sense, fluency with basic number combinations is a gradual process that grows out of rich number sense.

It is true that, direct instruction and drill of reasoning strategies and number facts can often promote accurate and efficient knowledge. However, Baroody argues that these approaches produce partial or limited fluency, and that guided discovery stands a better chance of promoting true fluency with both. That is, it better enables students to use reasoning strategies appropriately and flexibly (e.g., with previously unpracticed combinations) and also allows them to find a right answer quickly. When children are encouraged to discover mathematical regularities and to devise reasoning strategies for themselves—rather than being directly told—then they have a greater opportunity to develop conceptual understanding, strategic thinking, and a productive disposition toward learning and using mathematics.

Teachers Respond to the Research

Teachers were well aware of the importance of basic combination fluency in the early grades. During the seminar, however, they wrestled with a newer, expanded view of fluency, one that is in line with the National Research Council (2009) definition. While the teachers endorsed the value of strategic thinking and flexibility, many of them had questions about the relative importance of speed. They have been expected to measure and reward computational speed for so long that it was hard for them to imagine how to shift emphasis.

Speed and Fluency

The first two questions that Baroody answers address this nagging question of speed and the nature of what it means to "be fluent." One teacher marveled after the seminar, "What stands out to me is how incredibly inclusive the term *fluency* can be. It seems to be all things we associate with solid understanding and mastery. I personally became a bit lost." Other teachers also wondered about the relationship between fluency and general mathematical aptitude. **Is there a difference between "fast" and "efficient?" To what extent does speed matter? Can a student be fluent and still struggle at math? Can a student have success in math without fluency?**

Art Baroody's Response

I think of *fast* and *efficient* as interchangeable terms. And, yes, *ultimately*, speed matters because we want children to accurately and efficiently generate the basic sums and differences so they can, for example, use this knowledge to solve multiplication or division problems or multi-digit addition or subtraction problems.

However, fostering speed is secondary to promoting sensible or meaningful solutions. As William Brownell (1935) implied, premature emphasis on speed can undermine sense making (e.g., meaningful learning of relations and reasoning strategies), which is critical to other key aspects of fluency, namely appropriate and flexible application. Once children have devised counting or reasoning strategies of their own, they can be encouraged to use them efficiently or find even more efficient strategies.

The Common Core State Standards (Council of Chief State School Officers, 2010) suggest the following guidelines:

1. Kindergarteners should be able to use counting (Phase 1) strategies to determine sums and differences and be able to do so fluently with sums to 5 and their related differences.
2. First graders should be able to use counting (Phase 1) or reasoning (Phase 2) strategies to determine sums and differences up to 20 and be able to do so fluently with sums to 10 and their related differences. This includes knowing and using the subtraction-as-addition strategy.
3. Second graders should be able to use reasoning (Phase 2) strategies to add and subtract fluently within 20. By the end of the year, they should know all basic sums to 18 (Phase 3).

I think the kindergarten Common Core goals make sense if fluency with counting strategies means high accuracy and with *reasonable* efficiency—less than perhaps 5 seconds for small sums to 5 and more for larger sums. The grade 1 goals make sense if fluency with sums to 10 and their related difference means high accuracy within 3 seconds for relatively easy combinations and within about 6 seconds for the others. The grade 2 goal of recall of all sums to 18 is not supported by research and seems unrealistic, in my opinion. I believe that children in the second grade can achieve automatic reasoning strategies for the easiest sums (Phase 3) and accuracy with Phase 2 reasoning strategies for more difficult combinations.

Art Baroody's Response
As far as whether a student can be fluent and still struggle in math, or whether a student can have success in math without fluency, children can be fast and accurate with basic combinations because they have memorized them by rote. Such *partial* fluency, though, may not help children conceptually understand arithmetic, reason logically about numbers and numerical relationships, solve problems, or provide a basis on which to build future mathematical learning. Children who achieve true combination fluency have, by definition, a richer understanding of numbers and numerical relationships and are thus more likely to reason logically and be better problem solvers—be generally more successful at mathematics.

Guided Discovery Learning
The method of guided discovery learning was familiar to this group of early childhood teachers. For the most part, however, teachers had not thought about different types of discovery learning—"highly" versus "minimally" guided. They discussed the fact that many math learning opportunities are spontaneous and not the highly structured moments that can exist in a computer game. One spoke of how authentic problems were more likely to generate reasoning (i.e., problems such as *"How many pencils do we still need? How many kids are absent?"*), commenting, "that's where I hear the math conversation." Questions that emerged concerned the teacher's role in highly guided discovery learning, including the following: **Is there evidence to suggest that children are more likely to reason about number relationships in spontaneous problem solving situations than in structured activities?**

Art Baroody's Response

There is no doubt that *authentic problems* can provide invaluable opportunities for promoting meaningful conceptual learning and mathematical thinking. However, it's not always that simple. It comes down to whether children can assimilate (understand) the problem and have some (informal) means of solving it. If the problem is beyond their current developmental level or is not challenging, it may not serve a useful educational purpose. However, if the authentic problem is engaging to the students and if it poses a challenge just beyond a child's current developmental level, do take advantage of it! In fact, such problems are more likely to prompt and promote thinking and reasoning than stock textbook problems or computer drill programs. As a general rule, provide only as much guidance as absolutely needed.

How do children know how to use a known fact such as 5 + 5 to figure out a new fact, 5 + 6? What are examples of the teacher's role in highly guided instruction in the living, breathing, dynamic world of an early childhood classroom? Does the role of the teacher shift over time from preschool to second grade?

Art Baroody's Response

Children will only notice patterns and relations and use them to devise a reasoning strategy when they are developmentally ready to do so. For example, in order to discover the near-doubles reasoning strategy, a child needs to be reasonably fluent with two developmental prerequisites: (a) the doubles and (b) the number-after rule for adding 1. Children still using counting strategies with one or both prerequisites are unlikely to discover the near-doubles strategy or at least use it efficiently and perhaps accurately.

Teachers play a critical role in supporting guided discovery learning (see Baroody with Coslick, 1998, for a detailed discussion). These include:

◆ Assessing whether a child is developmentally ready to make a discovery

◆ Ensuring a steady stream of worthwhile problems that will foster learning and development

◆ Creating a community and climate of inquiry in which the emphasis of mathematics instruction is solving problems; looking for patterns and relations; sense making; sharing ideas and strategies; embracing conflicting ideas and evaluating them; and recognizing children's conjectures, ideas, and strategies by naming them after their originator (e.g., Kristin's conjecture, Roberto's rule, Nursel's strategy)

The general role of a teacher as a "guide on the side" (as opposed to a "sage on the stage") does not change in early childhood years. The roles described in the previous paragraph are applicable across Pre-K to Grade 2. What *does* change are the content goals for learning and the complexity of the problems to solve.

Practice That Promotes Reasoning

While the grades that the seminar participants taught (preschool to third) vary in their emphasis on fluent retrieval, there was strong consensus among teachers about the importance of promoting counting and reasoning strategies and ultimately their fluent use.

◆ *As a preschool teacher, it is important for my students to have lots of opportunity to compose and decompose numbers. I think the better they understand numbers, the better able they will be to think strategically about procedures to solve new problems.*

◆ *As I am teaching multiplication to my third graders, I see that my students go through the same three phases of developing fact fluency. They are beginning to think of what they already know (known facts) and use that to solve new problems.*

Several teachers shared examples of seeing children reason like this when they have compelling problems to solve. Teachers mentioned that children become familiar with some number combinations under 5 from experiences with *Five Little Monkeys Jumping on the Bed*. They noted how a familiar attendance routine can give children opportunities to reason about the number of children absent. However, even when these experiences are regular, they may not have the features of frequency or intensity that we might associate with fluency practice. So, teachers had questions about the nature of fluency practice, including: **What kind of fluency practice is most likely to develop relational thinking and be compelling for children? What features would need to be present in an activity in order for children to build fluency?**

Art Baroody's Response

The important point to keep in mind is that fluency is best promoted by *purposeful practice* (Baroody with Coslick, 1998). Purposeful activities are motivating to children. In addition to authentic problems, well-chosen projects and games can provide useful practice. Indeed, Carpenter et al. (1988) found that primary-grade students whose instruction focused on solving problems learned more basic combinations than those whose instruction focused on drill and practice. The researchers attributed the significant difference in no small part to the fact the problem-solving instruction was more engaging and entailed real use of the knowledge (i.e., was purposeful).

Are there differences between computer games designed for research and the kinds of games that should be played in classrooms or at home?

Art Baroody's Response

Computer games for research and teaching may have the same intended goal of increasing fluency. However, as research and teaching have different goals, the ways games are implemented may well differ.

- ◆ In a research study, it may be important to ensure children in different experimental conditions receive the same amount of practice exposure to a game in order to evaluate how this might impact whether a child achieved the goal immediately or not at all.

- ◆ In an educational setting (school, home, or online) the child would be able to play as long as needed to meet the learning goal.

Be aware, however, that not all computer games are designed to promote reasoning strategies. Many games offer unstructured drill and promote rote memorization. Such drill provides no structure or scaffolding. In contrast, computer games designed for guided discovery are structured to promote the discovery of a mathematical regularity. For example, presenting a series of problems such as 7 + 1, 7 + 2, 7 + 3. . . or 1 + 6, 2 + 5, 3 + 4. . . may embody a growing pattern and composition of seven, respectively. Once children have invented or learned a reasoning strategy meaningfully (Phase 2), practice is important to foster its efficient use (Phase 3). Carefully chosen computer games can be one effective way to provide this practice.

Assessment of Fluency

Teachers talked a lot about the pressure to get their students to master the basic facts and the anxiety that they and their students feel about it. One source of anxiety is timed tests, and the other is standardized tests. These final questions focus on assessment and related anxiety.

The computer interventions developed for research measured fluency rate with a timer. How did you approach timing children so as not to create anxiety?

Art Baroody's Response

There were three stages in the computer interventions, each phase lasted four weeks in the research condition. The timing was introduced in a developmentally appropriate manner, reflecting the focus of each stage.

- ◆ The first or conceptual stage was *untimed* and focused on discovery of a relationship. Also, in this first stage, practice was structured sequentially—that is, a helper item (*"After 4 comes?"*) was followed by a target item (*4 + 1 =*).

- ◆ The second or consolidation stage concentrated on reinforcing the relationship and on prompting the use of strategies with modest efficiency. At this point, timing was introduced but with a generous limit (children were given up to 6 seconds to respond). Half the practice was structured sequentially and half was not.

- ◆ The third stage focused on prompting the efficient use of a strategy and had a three second time limit. All practice was non-sequential.

In a classroom, a teacher should allow ample time for children to count and reason when arriving at their answers. Time limits can be gradually phased in to encourage greater and greater efficiency. Time limits are obviously inappropriate during Phase 1 (counting strategies) and should be generous in the Phase 2 (reasoning strategies). If used in such a developmentally appropriate manner and as a *challenge* for improving on a personal best, timed testing need not invoke overwhelming anxiety.

How can teachers advocate for giving students more time to develop basic fact fluency in meaningful ways when they—students and teachers—are measured against standardized tests that create pressure to go faster and cover more?

Art Baroody's Response

Although meaningful instruction may initially take more time, the fact is that in the long run it is more productive than scrambling to cover more content to pass a test. I think back to the experience I had in chemistry in high school, studying for the New York State Regents exam that determined my final grade. At the beginning of the school year, my chemistry teacher announced, *"I'm going to teach you chemistry my way* (meaningfully) *for three quarters and then we'll focus on preparing for the Regents exam in the last quarter."* As we had focused on the whys all year, cramming for the Regents exam was relatively easy. Instead of memorizing the answers to hundreds of meaningless questions, I found that I readily figured out answers to questions based on the understanding accrued over the life of the course. Similarly, meaningfully learning number combinations and building number sense will help primary grade students figure out high-stakes test questions better than merely trying to memorize definitions, procedures, and facts by rote. Not only will students be able to better apply their knowledge to novel problems; they will retain the knowledge better than learning it by rote. This will mean less review and more time for new, deeper instruction in the future. If all primary-level teachers in a school coordinate and work together to provide meaningful instruction, then there will be no need to cheat students by covering too much content, too fast, and too superficially.

Teachers' Ideas for Classroom Practice

The teachers in our group felt that the broader definition of number combination fluency makes teaching toward this goal more engaging for everyone. They had many ideas for promoting fluency development, shifting practices related to types of tasks and problems posed, the use of visual models to promote understanding, and methods of assessing fluency. They also thought of ways to send clear messages to families and other stakeholders about what fluency entails in the primary grades and how to help foster this at home.

Design Tasks and Problems That Help Children Notice Number Relationships

◆ *I think about the numbers I use for story problems and how carefully-chosen numbers can inspire children to use reasoning strategies. When I'm hoping to see my first graders use a "Make 10" strategy for example, I use lots of 9s and 11s in my story problems because it's likely that at least some of the kids will make a ten to add the numbers more easily.*

◆ *I use number talks daily. This routine is "highly guided discovery" in the sense that I start off with a known fact such as 6 + 6 to help them with the next problem of 6 + 7. We talk about how the first problem can help you with the next one.*

Purposeful task design and well-chosen numbers increase the likelihood that children will discover a reasoning strategy that will help them solve the problem at hand. This enables children to actively choose efficient strategies that are appropriate for their own level of understanding instead of passively relying on rote learning of the number combinations. Story problems in particular can be structured to draw attention to concepts such as composition and decomposition of numbers, place value, and the relationship between addition and subtraction. Story problems are also much more likely to engage and stimulate conversation and thinking than symbolic equations.

Number talks are another effective way to build fluency. Number talks involve mental math rather than paper and pencil drills, and they call for short classroom conversations around purposefully crafted computation problems (Parrish, 2010). Asking children to "do it in your head" makes it more likely they will use number relationships instead of memorized procedures. At the same time, inviting children to talk about their strategies gives them an opportunity to clarify their own thinking, justify their strategy, and learn about classmates' approaches.

Concept Box 6.2   Number Talks

The example number talk presented below is designed to focus first graders on the *near doubles* (or doubles plus/minus one) strategy. A teacher would use problems like these once students have a good understanding of the doubles facts (3 + 3 = 6; 4 + 4 = 8, and so on). The first problem activates this prior knowledge, and the sequence of problems encourages students to apply strategies from previous problems to subsequent, unknown problems.

First problem:

6 + 6

Teacher records:

Manny: I know it's 12 because it's like an egg carton. Two rows of 6.

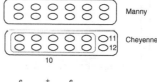 Manny

Teacher: I'll draw that. How would you count it?

Cheyenne: I would circle 10 in my head like a 10-frame and count 2 more.

Cheyenne

Zion: I did it different. I know that 6 is 5 and 1, so I put the two 5s together for 10 and the two 1s together for 2. That's 12.

Zion

Teacher: Does anyone see the numbers 5 and 1 on our egg carton drawing?

Henry: I see 5 and 1 on each row. If you cut the egg carton in half, the top has 5 and 1 and the bottom has 5 and 1.

Henry

Second problem:

7 + 6

Teacher records:

Gillian: I split 7 into 6 and 1 so it's the same problem plus 1.
Teacher: What do you mean, "it's the same problem?"

Gillian: It's 6 + 6 and 1 more.

Gillian

Christian: One more is 13.

Christian

Cameron: It's an egg carton plus an extra egg.

Cameron

Jason: It's 7 on top and 6 on the bottom.

Jason

Teacher: What's the number sentence?

$7 + 6 = 13$

Harper: 7 plus 6 equals 13.

Harper

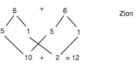
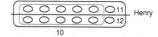
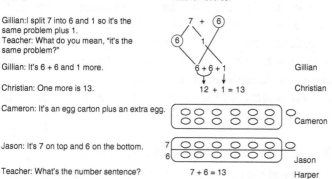

Use Visual Models

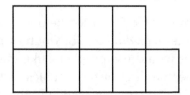

A ten-frame showing 4+5

◆ *Ten-frames help my first graders become fluent with combinations of 10. That visual helps them picture other relationships such as "4 + 5 is one missing from 10, or 9." So they are "seeing" other combinations in relation to the 10.*

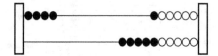

A rekenrek showing 6+10

◆ *We use a rekenrek (arithmetic rack) to build number sense and learn the basic facts. The kids seem to grasp doubles easily because of the two rows. Then the doubles-plus-one facts are easy to build to.*

◆ *When I am teaching multiplication, I start with visual representations such as equal groups and arrays. I always encourage children to think of what they already know (known facts) and use that to solve other problems.*

Young children are concrete learners, so visual models are a powerful way to help them see patterns and relationships in number combinations. The more children use visual models (such as *10-frames or rekenreks*), the more practice they have visually seeing—and gradually, mentally representing—the way that numbers can be composed and decomposed. They come to realize that they don't need to memorize a large number of discrete facts but can draw on these mental models to figure out harder combinations.

Assess True Combinational Fluency, Not Just Speed and Accuracy

◆ *I used to give timed tests to my second graders, but I stopped. The limited insight I gained from them just wasn't worth the sense of pressure they created.*

◆ *The main way I assess fluency is by observing my students play games. It's easy to see which strategies and facts they know and don't know.*

◆ *Number talks reveal a lot about students' flexibility and strategy selection. Are they picking a strategy that makes sense for that fact? Can they think about it in more than one way?*

◆ *I involve my students in assessing their own "fact power." They keep a chart of the addition facts to 10. They record whether they "just know it" or whether they used a strategy to solve it. They write the strategy's name from our anchor chart we've created as a class. They are proud to see their own progress over the year.*

The teachers we worked with embraced the idea that true fluency has more to do with meaning making than simply speed and accuracy. They find that if they want to assess flexibility, accuracy, efficiency, and appropriate use of strategies, they need to pay attention to what happens when children are engaged in activities, games, and reflection.

Enlist the Help of Families

◆ *One of my biggest challenges as a teacher is to work with students who do a lot of rote learning at home. They are so concerned with being correct that they take fewer risks and tend to be afraid to try new things because they don't want to be wrong or fail. This stifles their thinking and making connections. I use students' work samples to show parents that I value depth of knowledge and understanding, not just memorization.*

◆ *During conferences, I speak to families about the importance of students understanding their math facts rather than just memorizing. I notice a lot of parents are surprised to see there is a different way, and they are excited to know that their kids are going to become better mathematical thinkers compared to the ways they were taught.*

◆ *I have my students teach their parents these reasoning strategies so that they are aware of ways beyond flash cards to support their child's fact fluency.*

◆ *I encourage parents not to use flashcards but to incorporate math in their home. For example, when having children set the table, ask*

> *how many forks and knives are needed. If a parent is cooking, have the child add up the ingredients. This gives them practice, but in a meaningful context.*

◆ *I promote games. Playing simple games with dice and playing cards is a fun, low-stress way for children to practice their facts at home. I have "math backpacks" that families can check out with games, and I regularly send home copies of directions for the games we play in class.*

The teachers were sympathetic to parents' and other stakeholders' eagerness to help their children succeed at math and be prepared for the next level. However, they had observed that many families are likely to use rote methods at home, which the research literature, including that which is described in this chapter, does not support. The ideas described above are positive, proactive ways to communicate with families about the importance of more in-depth understanding of number relationships and ways to support this learning at home.

The Bottom Line

Baroody's research provides evidence for the theory that involving children in active meaning making (i.e., looking for patterns and relations and using the regularities found to solve problems) is more effective than rote memorization in supporting computational fluency. Furthermore, his results indicate that in terms of number combinations, highly guided discovery learning has unique beneficial effects on promoting active meaning making and fluency. In fact, "true fluency" with number combinations—evidenced by the ability to transfer knowledge to new problems—is, in most cases, best achieved through this type of instructional practice.

As we have seen, academic research studies must be rigorously designed to make sure that methods are carried out the same way for all subjects; for example, it is particularly important that the "dosage" or amount of practice is exactly the same for the intervention and the control groups. Therefore, for the purpose of research studies, the use of a carefully designed computer game is ideal. Further, computers can be programmed to provide a strategic sequence of problems to encourage discovery of a pattern or relationship and the construction of a reasoning strategy. As Baroody's research illustrates, structured or guided discovery learning is more effective than unstructured or unguided discovery (i.e., presenting a randomly sequenced practice problems)—except in the case of the highly noticeable *number-after* rule for adding 1.

However, even the best computer games can't capitalize on real problems that arise in a classroom, draw children's attention to them, and support children in finding solutions. It is classroom teachers who can point out situations that might involve certain reasoning strategies, and can create a context for a number talk that feels authentic to their particular classroom. Teachers also have the ability to be sensitive to children's gestures and body language as well as their spoken responses. They are present in the moment to orchestrate and facilitate questions and conversations and to provide positive feedback.

Further, well-informed teachers are in the best position to evaluate a child's readiness to learn new ideas. Reiterating Piaget, Baroody argues that the key to meaningful learning is not forming associations by rote but assimilating new information in terms of what is already understood. For primary-level educators, a key implication is that effective formal instruction builds on the (often considerable) informal mathematical knowledge young children bring to school. Put differently, the idea of constructing knowledge underscores the importance of educators taking into account a child's developmental readiness to understand and meaningfully learn a concept, procedure, or fact.

It takes many experiences over time for children to move from using counting, to using reasoning strategies, to knowing their facts. Games, story problems, number talks, and other activities that focus on noticing patterns and relations and using such regularities to invent reasoning strategies are effective for meaningfully memorizing the basic combinations. Practice that includes these kinds of activities will give children a more motivating and meaningful pathway to basic combination fluency.

Appendix

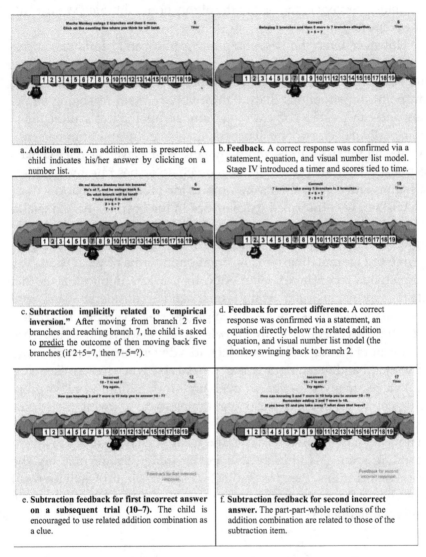

a. **Addition item**. An addition item is presented. A child indicates his/her answer by clicking on a number list.

b. **Feedback**. A correct response was confirmed via a statement, equation, and visual number list model. Stage IV introduced a timer and scores tied to time.

c. **Subtraction implicitly related to "empirical inversion."** After moving from branch 2 five branches and reaching branch 7, the child is asked to <u>predict</u> the outcome of then moving back five branches (if 2+5=7, then 7–5=?).

d. **Feedback for correct difference**. A correct response was confirmed via a statement, an equation directly below the related addition equation, and visual number list model (the monkey swinging back to branch 2.

e. **Subtraction feedback for first incorrect answer on a subsequent trial (10–7).** The child is encouraged to use related addition combination as a clue.

f. **Subtraction feedback for second incorrect answer.** The part-part-whole relations of the addition combination are related to those of the subtraction item.

Example feedback screens from highly-guided Mocha Monkey condition

Key Research Studies Discussed

Alfieri, L., Brooks, P. J., Aldrich, N. J., and Tenenbaum, H. R. (2011). Does discovery-based instruction enhance learning? *Journal of Educational Psychology, 103,* 1–18.

Baroody, A. J. (1987). The development of counting strategies for single-digit addition. *Journal for Research in Mathematics Education, 18,* 141–157.

Baroody, A. J. (2016). Reasoning and sense making in grades PK-2: Using number and arithmetic instruction as a basis for fostering mathematical reasoning. In M. T. Battista (Ed.), *Reasoning and sense making in the elementary grades.* Reston, VA: National Council of Teachers of Mathematics.

Baroody, A. J., with Coslick, R. T. (1998). *Fostering children's mathematical power: An investigative approach to K-8 mathematics instruction.* Mahwah, NJ: Lawrence Erlbaum Associates.

Baroody, A. J., Purpura, D. J., Eiland, M. D., and Reid, E. E. (2015). The impact of highly and minimally guided discovery instruction on promoting the learning of reasoning strategies for basic add-1 and doubles combinations. *Early Childhood Research Quarterly, 30,* 93–105.

Baroody, A. J., Purpura, D. J., Eiland, M. D., Reid, E. E., and Paliwal, V. (2016). Does fostering reasoning strategies for relatively difficult basic combinations promote transfer by K-3 students? *Journal of Educational Psychology, 108,* 576–591.

Brownell, W. A. (1935). Psychological considerations in the learning and the teaching of arithmetic. In W. D. Reeve (Ed.), *The teaching of arithmetic* (Tenth yearbook, National Council of Teachers of Mathematics, pp. 1–31). New York: Bureau of Publications, Teachers College, Columbia University.

Carpenter, T. P., Fennema, E., Peterson, P. L., and Carey, D. A. (1988). Teachers' pedagogical content knowledge of students' problem solving in elementary arithmetic. *Journal for Research in Mathematics Education, 19,* 385–401.

Council of Chief State School Officers. (2010). *Common Core State Standards: Preparing America's students for college and career.* Retrieved from www.corestandards.org/

National Research Council. 2009. *Mathematics learning in early childhood: Paths toward excellence and equity.* Washington, DC: The National Academies Press. https://doi.org/10.17226/12519. https://doi.org/10.17226/12519.

Parrish, S. (2010). *Number talks: Helping children build mental math and computation strategies, grades K-5.* Sausalito, CA: Math Solutions.

7

Math Anxiety and Math Performance: How Do They Relate?

Lisa Ginet and Rebeca Itzkowich, with Erin Maloney

Many people experience anxiety about math: a recent study found that 25% of students in four-year colleges and 80% of students in community colleges report moderate to high math anxiety. Interestingly, education majors are more likely to be math anxious than majors in other subjects, and early childhood and elementary education majors are more likely to be math anxious than other pre-service teachers (Chang & Beilock, 2016). Many preschool and kindergarten teachers have told us that they choose to teach younger children because they believe there is less math involved!

What is "math anxiety?" Math anxiety is defined as fear or stress about math. It is associated with lower math performance, and may result in an avoidance of everyday math-related tasks, such as calculating the tip at a restaurant. This makes sense, since research shows (and most people can attest) that any sort of fear or stress can interfere with cognition. In the United States, it is not unusual for people to claim that they "are not math people;" many of these people may have math anxiety. Since comfort with math is important, not only for school success but also for using numbers in everyday life, researchers have been working to understand the sources of math anxiety and identify strategies for reducing it.

In this chapter we interview Erin Maloney, a researcher at the Human Performance Lab at the University of Chicago. Maloney describes her work as "exploring cognitive and social factors that influence performance in mathematics and spatial processing." Maloney's work is influenced by her own experiences with math. In our interview with her, she recalled beginning to dislike math around ninth grade. She said, "For one reason or another, I started to believe that I simply was not a 'math person.' I knew that I was smart—just not 'math smart.' I would start to panic before any and all math tests, sometimes so much so that I would be sick to my stomach. I hated the idea of not being good at something, and I truly believed that I'd never be good at math." Maloney's own experience with math anxiety led to her interest in studying it when she became a cognitive psychologist. She wanted to focus on figuring out how math anxiety works, and whether people who are weak in mathematics compared to their peers also have more math anxiety.

What the Research Says

Math Anxiety and Math Performance: The "Chicken or Egg" Problem

When thinking about math anxiety and math performance, there is a "chicken or egg" problem. Which comes first: Do people who start out with weaker mathematical thinking skills become more mathematically anxious? Or do people start with math anxiety, which then "gets in the way" when they are trying to do math, leading to poor results? In one of her earliest studies, Maloney and her colleagues explored these questions. They wondered if weakness in early, basic mathematics skills might actually cause math anxiety in the first place.

To assess basic math skills, the researchers decided to look at people's ability to process *magnitude*. Magnitude refers both to the global sense of "more" and "less" (e.g., having a general sense of whether a number is more or less than another number) and to the development of an increasingly accurate mental number line (see Figure 7.1).

A young child's mental number line might be represented something like this.
As we learn more about magnitude and the number system, and we become more fluent and flexible using numbers, our mental number lines become more accurate.

Figure 7.1 Mental number line

Researchers have found that a solid sense of magnitude that continues to be refined is associated with strong numerical understanding and skills.

Working with undergraduate students, Maloney and her colleagues first measured their math anxiety levels. To do this, they asked respondents to rate the level of anxiety, on a scale from 1 to 5, that they experience in various situations—such as being given a "pop" quiz in a math class, reading a cash register receipt after a purchase, or walking into a math class. Using these survey results, they labeled participants as "high" or "low" in math anxiety.

To assess participants' abilities with numerical magnitude, they used two tasks. In the first experiment, participants were asked to report whether numerals 1 through 9 were lower or higher than 5. In the second experiment, participants decided which of two numerals represented the greater quantity (see Figure 7.2).

Although most people will answer these correctly, researchers can differentiate people's abilities with magnitude by measuring the time it takes to determine answers when numbers are close together (e.g., 5 and 6) versus far apart (e.g., 2 and 8). Everybody takes longer to answer when numbers are close together than when they are far apart, but people vary in *how much* longer. The difference is what researchers call the "numerical distance effect." The greater a person's numerical distance effect, the worse, it can be inferred, his magnitude skills.

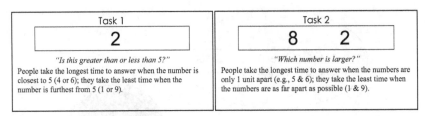

Figure 7.2 Two types of numerical magnitude tasks

In this study, Maloney and her colleagues found that the numerical distance effect was greater for people with high math anxiety than for people with low math anxiety. In other words, even on what are assumed to be very basic math tasks, people with higher math anxiety were performing worse. Further, in studies focusing on other kinds of math-related thinking, such as object counting and spatial thinking, Maloney and other researchers found similar results. Maloney said, "This kind of spawned the idea that maybe what's going on is that people who are high in math anxiety are actually starting with difficulties in some of the basic tasks. You can imagine that if you are a child coming to school with difficulties in counting, or magnitude representation, then you would actually end up doing worse in math, and that can lead you to be anxious about it."

The results above could indicate that, in the "chicken or egg" problem, weaker math abilities come first. However, when we interviewed Maloney, she said that a potential problem was that even though the task was designed to test basic math skills that should not cause anxiety, it is possible that for some people, anxiety still "got in the way" of performance. For example, it could be that simply seeing numerals made math-anxious people nervous, which made their responses slower.

Teacher Responses
◆ *This "chicken or the egg" problem has me thinking of different types of students. I am thinking of the ones who struggled due to not knowing the basic foundations of number sense or cardinality. Then I think of those who were deemed "smart" or "gifted" by another teacher or their parents. I've seen both groups have high math anxiety—for different reasons. The struggling student because he*

has no background knowledge or conceptual understanding to fall back on. The "gifted" student because he/she has this pressure from others to perform well—to live up to the label. So is it math anxiety which causes poor math performance in both these cases? Or in the case of the struggling students is their math anxiety caused by what they are lacking—foundational knowledge?

◆ *As a preschool teacher, I don't think I've identified "math anxiety." I see more often that children either have or do not have experience with math concepts. I do see students who feel they need to be "right" and only want to answer questions or work on problems they can easily solve. The anxiety becomes apparent when they are faced with something novel or something that involves more than rote memorization.*

◆ *I think the idea that people with weaker foundations would develop higher math anxiety makes sense, because often the foundations are taught and related to speed with which students can solve and get the answers. The "answer" is the end goal. If someone's mental memory capacity is quicker than others', then that person is successful and the others around them don't have the opportunity to be successful, especially in a classroom setting. That immediately creates a "winner and the rest" scenario in a group of children.*

Math Anxiety and Problem-Solving Strategies in Children

To try to better understand the relationship between mathematics skills and the development of math anxiety, Maloney turned her attention to young children. Although studies have found that children as young as six can suffer from math anxiety, there is much to be learned about how it begins developing by exploring it in these early years—before years of school-math difficulties and fears build up. In this study, Maloney and her colleagues investigated problem-solving strategies in first and second graders.

The researchers asked children to complete three different assessments to measure their math anxiety level, working memory (Concept Box 7.1), and math problem solving strategies. Math anxiety was assessed in a similar way as described earlier, but with statements more relevant to children (e.g., to rate how they feel when a teacher calls on them to explain a math problem on the board), and by having children point to faces that showed expressions ranging from, as explained to the children, "not nervous at all" to "very very nervous." Working memory was assessed using both forward and backward letter-span recall (Concept Box 7.1). To assess students' problem solving strategies, researchers read a number story problem aloud to the children, such as "If you had nine crayons and someone gave you eight more, how many would you have altogether?" The researchers watched to see what sorts of strategies the children used to solve the problem, and also asked the children how they solved the problem. They did not provide manipulatives so that children would be more likely to talk through their strategies.

Concept Box 7.1   What Is Working Memory?

"Working memory" describes the cognitive system through which we store and manage the visual and auditory information that we use at any given time to complete a task. To take a math example, if we were to figure out how much change we should get from a 20 dollar bill for a $14.59 item, we would be using our working memory to store all the numbers while we complete the steps of the problem. Working memory is often tested by asking people to recall unrelated strings of letters or digits, sometimes forward and sometimes backward, starting with a 2- or 3-item string, and then giving longer strings until two in a row are wrong. Most people's working memory is between 5 and 7 letters or digits.

Maloney and her colleagues reviewed the children's strategies, classifying them according to type, and evaluating the types as more or less advanced. The strategies they observed are listed in Table 7.1. It is important to note that more advanced strategies rely on more working memory. It takes more memory, for example, to remember the steps within the decomposition strategy or to retrieve the correct answer than to count on one's fingers. Thus, children with more working memory capacity will be more likely to successfully use the more advanced strategies.

Table 7.1 Types of strategies children used to solve number story problems

Sample Problem: If you had nine crayons and someone gave you eight more, how many would you have altogether?

Strategy	Example	Description
Counting	Child says, "9," then counts on, "10, 11, 12, 13, 14, 15, 16, 17," using fingers to keep track. "I counted."	Less advanced; less working memory required
Weak retrieval (answer more than 1 unit away)	Child says, "9 plus 8, that's 13." "I knew it."	Less advanced; less working memory required
Guessing	Child says, "15? 20?" "I'm not sure."	Less advanced; less working memory required
Strong retrieval (answer within 1 unit of correct)	Child says, "9 plus 8, that's 17." "I knew it."	More advanced; more working memory required
Decomposition	Child says, "9 and 1 more make 10, then there's 7 more, and 7 and 10 are 17." "I figured it out."	More advanced; more working memory required

The researchers found an interesting intersection among math anxiety, working memory, and math performance (Table 7.2). For children with low working memory, performance was relatively poor, regardless of math anxiety. However, for children with high working memory, the more math anxious the children were, the worse their math performance. Why would this be? To understand this better, the researchers examined the strategies that the children used to solve the problems. They found that level of math anxiety was linked to the types of strategies used, but that the relationship was different for children with high versus low working memory. Specifically, of children with high working memory, those who were highly math-anxious were less likely to make use of more advanced strategies than those who were less math-anxious. Children with low working memory available used less sophisticated strategies and had lower math performance, regardless of their levels of math anxiety.

What does all of this mean? The results suggest that math anxiety interferes with the use of working memory. Children with high working memory should be able to use more sophisticated problem-solving strategies, but high math anxiety keeps them from using

Table 7.2 Strategy use and performance of children with different levels of math anxiety and working memory

	High working memory	Low working memory
High math anxiety	Used less sophisticated strategies; performed worse	Used less sophisticated strategies; performed worse
Low math anxiety	Used **more** sophisticated strategies; performed **better**	Used less sophisticated strategies; performed worse

Note: Only children with both high working memory *and* low math anxiety were able to use more sophisticated strategies.

these strategies. Going back to the chicken or egg problem, this study suggests that anxiety may actually be "getting in the way" of children's math performance, at least for those children with high working memory.

Teacher Responses
◆ Sometimes students will choose one answer and then see a fellow student has a different answer. Then they will change their answer and be unable to explain why. Other students are comfortable choosing and sticking with their answer even though everyone else has a different answer. Sometimes they are right, sometimes they are wrong, but they stick to their answer.

◆ In my own experience teaching, it seems that the preschoolers who are more self-aware (aware of their actions, able to have conversations with teachers and peers) are more likely to "shut down" and not attempt to think about a challenging math problem or situation than their peers who may be less self-aware. Those who are less self-aware are more likely to openly and energetically take guesses and not be affected by their incorrect answer. Does this mean "smarter" students are more susceptible to math anxiety?

Parent and Teacher Math Anxiety, and Its Relation to Children's Math Achievement and Anxiety

In another study, Maloney and her colleagues investigated the source of math anxiety. They knew from previous studies that some children have math anxiety as early as first grade. Where is it coming from? Have they already experienced difficulties in math that led them to be anxious? Are they "catching" math anxiety from the adults around them? To try to answer these questions, the researchers explored the relationship between children's math anxiety, math achievement, and their *parents'* math anxiety. In the study, first and second graders completed math achievement tests and a math anxiety questionnaire at the beginning and end of the school year. Additionally, the children's parents completed math anxiety questionnaires as well as surveys asking how often they helped their children with their math homework.

The researchers found that children with parents who were highly math-anxious and who often helped with math homework showed both less math learning than expected over the course of the year *and* higher math anxiety at the end of the year. On the other hand, children whose parents had low math anxiety did not show these results. Further, children who had highly math-anxious parents who *did not* often help them with math homework did not show these results (see Table 7.3). These results suggest that children can "catch" math anxiety from their parents. However, the math anxiety of the parents is not just "in the air" for the children to catch. Rather, the math anxiety seems to be brought out when parents help their children with math homework. This increases the children's own anxiety and decreases their learning.

In a similar study, Sian Beilock—also a developmental psychologist at the University of Chicago—and her colleagues looked into the way that *teachers'* math anxiety might influence their students' achievement. They measured first and second grade teachers' math anxiety at

Table 7.3 Children's learning and math anxiety as related to amount of homework help by parents with high and low math anxiety

	Parents help with homework often	Parents don't help with homework often
Parents with high math anxiety	Children show **less than typical** math learning and **higher math anxiety** at end of year	Children show typical math learning and math anxiety stays the same
Parents with low math anxiety	Children show typical math learning and math anxiety stays the same	Children show typical math learning and math anxiety stays the same

Note: Only children whose parents both had high math anxiety and helped with math homework showed less math learning and higher math anxiety.

the beginning of the school year, and students' math achievement at the end of the year. They found that the teachers' math anxiety was related to students' math achievement, but *only for the girls*. That is, the more math anxious the teacher, the worse the girls' math achievement. The boys' math achievement was not affected by the teachers' anxiety.

Why would the teachers' anxiety only affect the girls? First, all of the teachers in the study were female. Second, the researchers found that girls who had math-anxious teachers were also more likely, at the end of the school year, to agree with the statement that "boys are good at math and girls are good at reading." The students that agreed with this statement tended to do worse in math. Beilock and her colleagues concluded that the girls picked up on the math anxiety of their female teachers and began to believe that girls are not good at math.

Teacher Responses

◆ *I find it interesting that girls can pick up math anxiety from their teacher. Makes me wish I could go back and do it all again with some of my students. Makes me wonder how they are now. Do they continue to have math anxiety issues?*

◆ *I remember having parents tell me, "I wasn't good in math when I was in school." I also remember parents throwing their hands up at conferences saying they don't know how to help their children with math at home. So I can see where if parents have math anxiety and the children sense this when they need help at home, the anxiety can be transferred to the child.*

◆ *I was one of those teachers! My students' data always showed tremendous growth in reading but steady growth in math. I hated math in high school and college. It wasn't until I got involved in math work in my district that I made some shifts in my instruction and saw great results.*

◆ *It is sad to see that teachers with math anxiety can negatively impact their female students. I would hope the opposite is also true—that teachers who love math will positively impact all their students.*

Family Math App and Children's Math Achievement

The research so far does not solve the "chicken or egg" question as to high math anxiety and math learning difficulties; it may well be the case that either could come first, and the origin might be different for different people. Regardless, once either is established, high math anxiety and math learning difficulties continue to affect each other, in the lives of both individuals and families. Is it possible to disrupt that cycle? Are there ways to help parents help their children with math that both decrease anxiety and increase understanding? To try to answer that question, Maloney and her colleagues investigated whether using an educational iPad application designed to get parents and children talking about math could increase children's math achievement.

In this study, families of first graders were given an iPad Mini that included an app. Some families received the original math version of the free app, called "Bedtime Math." The app displays a passage each day about a variety of topics, and related math questions for different age levels—"Wee ones," "Little kids," and "Big kids" (see Figure 7.3). Other families received a modified version of the app that focused on reading instead of math. The reading version provided similar passages to the math app but did not include any numerical or spatial content. Families were free to use the app they received as often as they liked. To assess children's gains and the relation to parents' math anxiety, the researchers assessed children's math achievement at the beginning and end of the study, as well as parents' math anxiety. They also had access to data about how often the families used the apps.

Figure 7.3 Sample passage and related math questions from Bedtime Math app

It's *National Doughnut Day* in America, which might be our best holiday yet. This sweet treat was invented in the 1800s, when a sailor's mom, Elizabeth Gregory, was trying to fry cakes more evenly. Sometimes the outside of the cake would cook too much before the inside did, leaving it goopy and yucky in the middle. To solve the problem, she put a wad of walnuts in the middle of the ball of dough. Since she wrapped dough around a nut, she called it a "dough-nut." Now America eats *billions* of doughnuts every year. The Salvation Army started National Doughnut Day in 1938, as a thank-you to women who served doughnuts to soldiers. They put the holiday on the first Friday of June, and we still celebrate it today . . . but thankfully, we can eat doughnuts any day of the year.

Questions to help your child find the math in this story

◆ *Wee ones:* What shape is a donut?

◆ *Little kids:* If you order 2 chocolate donuts, 2 sugar-glazed, and 2 cinnamon, how many donuts do you have? *Bonus:* What is the latest day in June that National Doughnut Day can happen?

◆ *Big kids:* People always eat up the chocolate donuts faster. If you serve 18 donuts, all chocolate or powdered, how many should be chocolate if you want twice as many chocolate as powdered? *Bonus:* If instead you put out 3 dozen donuts, and want the same number of powdered and jelly, but as many chocolate as the powdered and jelly put together, now how many of each do you need?

Answers

* *Wee ones:* A circle—or in 3D, a "torus."

* *Little kids:* 6 donuts. *Bonus:* On June 7. Starting June 8, the day would be the second Friday.

* *Big kids:* 12 chocolate, leaving you 6 powdered. *Bonus:* 18 chocolate, 9 powdered and 9 jelly.

Not surprisingly, the researchers found that children's math achievement was not related to how often the families who received the reading app used it. However it was a different story with those who received the math version: the more that families did math together with the app, the greater the gains in children's math achievement. What is most interesting about the study's results, however, is that this increase in math achievement was larger in children whose parents were highly math anxious. In other words, it was those children who were most at risk of underachieving—those whose parents were high in math anxiety—that ended up gaining the most from the math app.

Why did the Bedtime Math app help? The researchers hypothesized that it provided ways for parents to talk to children about math. They wrote, "The app may give parents—especially high-math-anxious parents or even parents with less skill or interest in engaging in math—more and better ways to talk to their children about math not only during app usage but also in other everyday interactions." Thus, providing a vehicle for talking to kids about math may be a way to help break the cycle of high math anxiety and low math achievement.

Teacher Responses

- ◆ *I like that the app wasn't so much about finding an answer to a problem, but a conversation starter for parents. I would like to think that parents would see how you can easily add math to the conversation in ways that don't provoke anxiety for themselves or their children. It would be interesting to see if there was an increase in the use of math language in these households after using this app on a regular basis.*

- ◆ *I wonder why using the app was different from helping with homework. Does the pressure of homework being evaluated by the teacher increase the anxiety?*

Conclusion

Erin Maloney's research into math anxiety shows that it is not a simple phenomenon. She and her colleagues have discovered some ways that math anxiety and math performance are related. For example, math anxiety seems to be related to very basic skills such as comparing numbers (magnitude assessments). For more complex problems, math anxiety may get in the way by interfering with a person's tendency to use strategies that involve high working memory. Further, parents' math anxiety may increase children's math anxiety and lower their math achievement. However, there are ways to help highly math-anxious parents support their children's math learning.

Maloney's story itself offers hope for people who are math anxious. She described how she started to like math when she became interested in psychology, which required learning about statistics.

> I knew psychology required mathematics, but I was fascinated by the idea of conducting research in psychology and the concept of being able to ask a question and, for some amount of time after I analyzed the data, being the only person in the entire world who knew the answer to that question. As I fell more and more in love with research, I began using statistics more and more, and, almost without realizing it, I found myself really enjoying conducting calculations and working with numbers. Interestingly, for me, even though what I was doing was absolutely math, it never *felt* like math in that I really enjoyed it! Towards the end of graduate school I finally accepted that maybe there was no such thing as 'math people' and that I really did enjoy math!

Teachers Respond to the Research

When a group of teachers gathered to discuss this research, we asked them to consider the ways that their own math learning experiences and social identities have affected their attitudes and beliefs about teaching math. We called these their "math autobiographies." Teachers talked about their varying levels of math anxiety and how they think this influenced choices they made in their lives. Given their own experiences with math anxiety and their observations of students with math anxiety, they were not surprised to read about the prevalence of the issue and the correlation between math anxiety and math performance. They raised several important points in response to the research and its implications for classroom practices. We describe these below, followed by Erin Maloney's responses.

Math Anxiety at Different Ages and Grade Levels

Teachers shared their observations about their own students' anxiety at different grade levels. "I teach preschool. They don't have math anxiety." So stated one of the teachers, who felt that young children might be stressed or risk-averse, but that the discomfort is diffuse. Another teacher, in kindergarten, said, "I don't think there's math anxiety at this age because there's still a lot of exploratory play involved . . . then, in first grade, it turns into 'I have to do good because I'm going to be taking a test.'" A former third grade teacher talked about parents being concerned that their children were suddenly struggling in math and getting more anxious. These observations led to questions about the relationship between math anxiety and age or grade level:

How early does math anxiety start? Is there evidence of math anxiety as young as preschool? How does math anxiety change as children get older and school math changes?

Erin Maloney's Response

These questions are really great questions, and they are ones that my colleagues and I have been working to answer. As of right now we do not know the full developmental trajectory of math anxiety. We have seen math anxiety in children as young as first grade, and this anxiety is linked to their math performance (such that higher anxiety is linked to lower math achievement). There are no published studies to date that have looked at math anxiety in preschoolers, so I can't really say whether children this age experience math anxiety.

Most of the published research suggests that math anxiety likely increases over time until children are in late middle school or early high school. It is believed that, after that point, it plateaus. Because there have not been any studies to date that follow children from preschool through to adulthood and assess math anxiety, we cannot be completely certain of this hypothesized pattern, but, given the cross-sectional data the we do have, it is our "best guess" that math anxiety starts around first grade, increases until late middle school or early high school, and then plateaus.

Who experiences math anxiety, and how?

Another common theme in the teacher discussion was how different types of learners may be more or less susceptible to developing math anxiety. A child may have speech delays that make it difficult to interact with others; a child may be learning multiple languages and have a limited vocabulary in the classroom's dominant language; a child may have developmental delays that interfere with the ability to work productively with peers. In all of these cases, there might be generalized anxiety that could mask or amplify math-specific anxiety, leading teachers to ask: **How does the prevalence and appearance of math anxiety relate to different individual characteristics of learners?**

Erin Maloney's Response

This is another really important question. However, there has not been a great deal of work done in this area. Research has shown that students who are anxious in general are more likely to have math anxiety. I am, however, unaware of any research examining characteristics such as learning multiple languages, or having a speech delay and how these may relate to math anxiety. I do think that this is an important and interesting area or future research.

Testing Stress and Math Anxiety

Teachers brought up anxiety generated by tests—both curriculum based and "high-stakes" tests. They felt that many of their students experienced stress due to the high-stakes testing environment in their schools, even when the students were not the test-takers. (Preschoolers, kindergartners, and primary students rarely participate in school-wide tests, but often have to deal with rallies, announcements, and changes in school routines during testing periods.) They wondered how (or whether) to distinguish between stress about taking tests and math anxiety. This discussion leads to two questions: **Could high stakes testing cause (or increase) math anxiety? Has research found that there are some children who only experience math anxiety during tests but not in other contexts?**

Erin Maloney's Response

It is certainly true that people can experience anxiety during high-stakes tests (for a really great book that discusses this phenomenon, I recommend reading *Choke* by Sian Beilock). In research we often discuss "Math anxiety" as something different from "Test anxiety." In truth, the ways in which these two different anxieties manifest seem to be quite similar, and as such, we hypothesize that they would likely respond similarily to the same treatments. Differentiating math anxiety from test anxiety becomes important when we are working to understand how they come about. I believe that there are cognitive factors (e.g., difficulty with number processing, difficulty with spatial processing) that can pre-dispose a student to develop math anxiety.

I would not suggest that these same cognitive factors would predispose a student to develop anxiety about tests in general.

Mindset and Math Anxiety

Teachers were interested in the difference between general anxiety and math anxiety in particular, and what this means for helping children in their classroom. Many of the teachers were aware of the idea of "growth mindset" (Concept Box 7.2). Some teachers also mentioned that they thought that helping children develop a growth mindset might reduce all sorts of learning anxiety. The teachers wanted to know: **How much of math anxiety is related to general anxiety or self awareness/willingness to take risks? Is there research on the relationship between growth mindset and anxiety? On a practical level, should teachers be trying to identify who has math anxiety in particular, or should the goal be to lessen students' anxiety in general?**

Erin Maloney's Response

This is a really great and really complex question. I will answer it by breaking it down into a few parts. Firstly, while there is a relation between math anxiety and general anxiety, not all of math anxiety can be explained by anxiety in general. In other words, to a large extent math anxiety is still separate from general anxiety. As far as I know right now, there has not been any research published on the relation between math anxiety and growth mindset, but this is an area that my colleagues and I are very interested in, and we are currently working to unpack this relation.

With respect to whether teachers should be targeting math anxiety or anxiety more generally: because math anxiety, test anxiety, and general anxiety all tend to manifest as negative thoughts and ruminations that occupy cognitive resources, and because these anxieties will likely all respond somewhat similarly to the same treatments, it is likely more effective to work on teaching students anxiety reduction techniques in general. Two of my favorite anxiety-reduction techniques (which I've advocated to the students that I teach as well as use regularly in my own day-to-day life) are (1) focused breathing and (2) expressive writing. With focused breathing, it can be as simple as placing your hand on your belly, closing your eyes, and breathing deeply for a few long breaths. With expressive writing, you can simply write about your anxieties about an upcoming test, exam, assignment, for 5 to 7 minutes. Both focused breathing and expressive writing have been demonstrated to be effective techniques at reducing anxiety in general and at reducing the negative consequences of math anxiety on math performance, leading to increased math performance.

Concept Box 7.2   What Is "Growth Mindset?"

Psychologist Carol Dweck has studied and popularized the idea of "growth mindset" and "fixed mindset." She argues that people who have a growth mindset believe that intelligence, cognition, and abilities can develop through effort, experimentation, and persistence; people with a fixed mindset feel these are unchangeable qualities. People who have a growth mindset are more likely to take on risks and learn deeply than people with a fixed mindset, who may decide that they are not good at a skill and that no amount of work will change that. A person's mindset is not the same at all times or in all content areas. Other people's expectations and reactions can affect one's attitude and mindset, and teachers can be intentional about creating a growth-inspiring culture in the classroom.

Working Memory, Task Selection, and Math Anxiety

The teachers were intrigued by the interaction between working memory and math anxiety in the study of children's use of strategies. This led to a discussion of the working memory and comprehension demands of different sorts of mathematical tasks. For example, some math tasks are presented visually, some with concrete objects, some with words (oral or written). A math problem may be part of a real-world situation, or it may be presented out of context with symbols only. These features of tasks may require different levels of working memory. The group asked: **Does the type of task, and therefore level of working memory required, affect math anxiety? Are there other ways in which type of task influences math anxiety?**

Erin Maloney's Response

This is an area of research in which we need to do more work. I think that this is a very interesting question, and many people are working hard to unpack how different question-types vary in terms of cognitive demand, but to date, there has not been a large amount of research conducted exploring how all of these factors relate to math anxiety.

Math Anxiety at Home

Early childhood teachers work hard to build connections between school and home. The discussion of the two studies involving parents led this group to wonder: **Can teachers reduce parents' math anxiety? Could the type of math work sent home affect parents' math anxiety, which in turn might influence level of math anxiety in the child?**

Erin Maloney's Response

This is an avenue of research in which I am particularly interested. There really hasn't been much work done of which I am aware looking into these issues. However, I will say that I think it is very important for parents to be as involved in their children's education as they can be. As such, I think strong communication between teachers and parents is needed regarding: the types of questions the children are receiving; the strategies that are being taught in the classrooms; why these strategies may be different from how the parents learned; and why we believe that these strategies are more effective than the strategies used when many of us went through school. It is my own personal belief that keeping these doors of communication open as much as possible could go a long way in terms of creating a positive learning environment for the students, the parents, and the teachers.

Teachers' Math Anxiety

The teachers were thinking carefully about what they project in the classrooms, and wanted to know how they can assess their own beliefs about math and what kinds of messages they are sending to their students. They hope the research might have advice for them: **How can teachers measure or reduce their own math anxiety?**

Erin Maloney's Response

For the most part, we tend to have a pretty good idea of how anxious we are about math. You can simply ask yourself, "In general, how nervous do I feel when engaging with math"? If you think that you may be anxious about math then I suggest working to implement some of the anxiety-reduction strategies mentioned above (e.g., focused breathing and expressive writing). Regardless of whether a teacher is anxious about math or not, I think that it is very important to work to communicate to students that math is important, it is useful, anyone can learn it if they work at it (i.e., there isn't such a thing as a "math person" and "not a math person"), and that it can be a really fun and rewarding subject area. As educators, it is important that we work to create a positive learning environment for students and that we realize that strategies that work for one student may not work for another and that that's OK—we can work at it until we find a strategy that is effective.

Teachers' Ideas for Classroom Practice

In their discussion of the research about math anxiety, teachers considered how to apply the findings to their work with children and families. They shared approaches that they already use in the classroom and discussed new ideas as well. Their thoughts are summarized below.

Work to Establish a Positive, "Growth-Focused" Learning Community

- *In my own classroom I really strive to create an environment where children are comfortable taking chances in expressing their thinking and where children understand that we are all learning together.*

- *As teachers, we need to be enthusiastic about what we're teaching our students. Create opportunities to wonder aloud about how to solve problems. Make mistakes in front of the children, and demonstrate resilience and persistence.*

- *I am a firm believer in the power of language. To prevent math anxiety, I try to speak about mathematical work in a growth-mindset perspective. I avoid talking about math abilities, or any academic abilities for that matter, as fixed. For example, saying something like, "Wow, that's a question that will make your brain grow," rather than, "Oh, that problem is hard." A problem being hard is not changeable, but a question that makes your brain grow is manageable and able to be attempted.*

Teachers can do a lot to foster a positive mathematical learning environment. Pose problems that do not have an immediately obvious solution; then encourage peer cooperation and collective effort. Watch for and make use of mistakes, as they provide the most fertile ground for learning (see Figure 7.4 for an example). Ask children to share their thinking through posters or journals; then they can see the ideas and strategies they are developing over time. The goal of these practices is for children to see math as an activity that everyone can participate in.

It's spring time in a second grade classroom. The teacher has used number strings all year to build children's fluency and flexibility with arithmetic. The children quickly answer the "helper problem" (a beginning problem designed to be relatively easy and to activate ideas that can help children solve the next problem) and move on to the next.

100 – 80 = 20 (helper problem)
102 – 79 =

After a few moments of quiet thought, the teacher calls on two children who have given a "thumbs up" to indicate they have an answer. One child says the answer is 22, and the other child says the answer is 23. There are children who signal "me, too" to each answer.

The teacher asks one of the children who said 22 to explain how he solved it. As the child talks, the teacher uses an open number line (see illustration) to model the solution:

Child: *I hopped from 79 to 80 because that's an even 10. . .*
Teacher draws:

Child: *Then I know 80 to 100 is 20 and 2 more is 22.*
Teacher draws:

Child: *Oh! I forgot about hopping 1 to get to 80. . . the answer's 1 more—23!*
Teacher draws:

A lot of children are nodding their heads, and the teacher says, "The open number line can help us keep track when we're figuring out the difference between two numbers—how far apart they are."

Figure 7.4 Make use of mistakes!

As mentioned before, many teachers have found ideas about mindset (Concept Box 7.2) to be particularly relevant to learning math, especially in our society, where it is considered acceptable to say, "I am not a math person" (a fixed mindset perspective!). If teachers promote a growth mindset in the classroom, then there is likely to be less math anxiety, because math activities are viewed as something to work on and learn from, not as something that only some people are inherently good at. Teachers promote a growth mindset not only by choosing what they say to children who are struggling, but also by building a positive, growth-focused community of learners.

Engage Children in Meaningful Mathematical Thinking

◆ *I try to use language that calls attention to the mental work the children are doing and highlights those skills, as opposed to praising a right answer at the end of the situation. Hopefully if children's first experiences in school are in this type of environment, they will feel excited to tackle different types of mathematical situations and enjoy the process of solving and figuring out more than the praise of a right answer.*

◆ *I think it's important, after children give their answers, to ask follow-up questions such as, "How did you know that?" and praise the problem solving/thinking process rather than the correctness of the answer.*

Engaging children in meaningful mathematical thinking is another strategy for reducing math anxiety. Teachers can do this by helping children to develop the skills to share their thinking, justify their reasoning, and productively critique the thinking and reasoning of others. One way to help them develop these skills is to demonstrate the behavior, by "thinking aloud" when solving a problem. Another way is to provide them with sentence stems such as . . . "When I looked at the problem, it reminded me of . . . " or "I disagree because . . . " These can be a useful starting place for young children. When the focus is on the process that leads to solutions and not on who has the right answer, children may experience less anxiety.

Some teachers also suggest that using a pen instead of a pencil for math work can support children's thinking. When students use a pen, the thinking that went into any erroneous paths is preserved. This focuses everyone on the importance of the *process* of mathematical thinking, rather than on the need to come to a correct *solution*.

Avoid Timed Arithmetic Tests

◆ *In my earlier years of teaching, I used timed tests to assess children's fluency on beginning operations, such as "4 + 1." In retrospect, there were certainly kids who were generally "good students" who would freeze up and not do well on these assessments. At the time, I think I believed I was helping to prepare them for the future timed tests that would surely come in later grades. Now I fear that I was also helping to build math anxiety.*

Teachers have long relied on timed arithmetic tests because they feel that such exercises are the only way for children to prove that they "know their facts." However, many teachers have noticed that timed arithmetic tests cause anxiety in their students—even those students who don't display math anxiety in other situations. There are other ways to encourage children to use and make sense of number relationships and build their fluency in arithmetic. If timed test sheets come with your curriculum, consider using them in other ways. Some teachers ask children to write down the answers they "just know" with one color; then use a different color to answer others that they can figure out. Other teachers cut up the number sentences and ask children to put them in groups that are related.

Play Math Games

◆ *One of the most powerful things we have done in our classroom to help children enjoy math is to play math games. Because playing "memory" with dot cards is fun, kids want to do this on their own, and I have seen their fluency with number composition—the idea that four can be one and three or two and two—increase.*

Math games provide meaningful situations for children to apply mathematical ideas and skills. When choosing math games, teachers should look for those that focus on an important idea, and are also easy to learn to play, such as "Capture," "Matching Pairs," "NIM," "Mancala," or "21." When children are learning a game, the teacher can play with

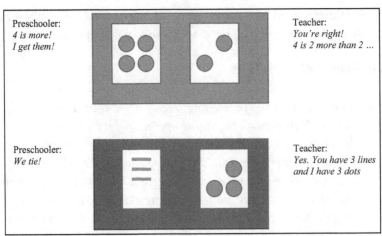

"Capture" can vary in mathematical complexity:
– The quantities represented in the cards can be smaller or larger.
– Players can each draw one card or draw two cards and add (or multiply) the quantities.

"Capture" is a card game usually played with two people. The cards have quantities of dots, lines, and other images represented on them. Each player has a pile of cards face down. Both players turn over the top card, and whoever has the card with more captures the pair of cards.

Figure 7.5 The Math Game "Capture"

them and model language to describe the math that is going on. (See Figure 7.5 for an example of a math game.)

Games reduce anxiety and promote positive attitudes toward math because they reduce the fear of failure and error, since children can always play again. It can be helpful to provide children with a model of what to do when they win or lose, so the focus stays on the fun of playing—winners can give two thumbs up and say "Yes!" with quiet enthusiasm; losers can shrug their shoulders and say "Oh well."

Encourage Family Involvement in Children's Math Learning

◆ *Parents who are anxious about math sometimes need help thinking about how they can talk with their child about the math they deal with in their everyday life. I would like parents to see that they can easily add math to their everyday conversations in ways that don't provoke anxiety for themselves or their children.*

◆ *I plan to have parents learn one of the games we play in the classroom, and to give them specific sentence starters for conversations around math, such as "I wonder how many. . . ?"*

◆ *For the first 10 minutes of every day, the majority of our parents enter the classroom with their children and read together on the carpet. It's a beautiful time that families spend together in the classroom, building our learning community. On Fridays we have been doing special activities that may revolve around story dictation, creating book recommendations, doing identity activities, and now I would like to place a priority on having a math activity or exploration available where we can teach them games that encourage math conversations.*

When teachers host family math nights where parents and children read math-related books, solve math problems, and play math games together, then they are giving families the tools to engage children in mathematical conversations. Parents and children can take math games and other meaningful math activities or math conversation starters home with them. These provide frameworks for home math learning that are high in meaning, but low in stress.

Find Ways to Have Fun With Math Yourself

◆ *This research will influence my teaching. I will place a higher priority on sharing my own experiences with math in my daily life in a confident manner. I want to help the children, especially the girls, see themselves as strong mathematicians. If I can exude this myself, hopefully they will see it as a truth for themselves too.*

In order to reduce math anxiety in children, teachers need to reduce it in themselves, as well. One way to do this is to find or create a community of learners at the school or district level who are committed to learning about math together. Teachers, parents, and administrators can read a book together and use it as the basis for conversation and study. Here are some suggestions:

5 Practices for Orchestrating Productive Mathematics Discussions, by
   M. K. Stein & M. S. Smith (N.C.T.M., 2011)
Beyond Answers, by M. Flynn (Stenhouse, 2017)
*Big Ideas of Early Mathematics: What Teachers of Young Children
   Need to Know*, by Erikson Institute's Early Math Collaborative
   (Pearson, 2014)

*Mathematical Mindsets: Unleashing Students' Potential Through
   Creative Math, Inspiring Messages and Innovative Teaching*, by
   J. Boaler (Jossey-Bass, 2016)
*Young Mathematicians at Work: Constructing Number Sense,
   Addition & Subtraction*, by C. T. Fosnot & M. Dolk (Heinemann,
   2001)

Another way for teachers to become less anxious about math is to find games or puzzles that are both enjoyable and mind-stretching, as well as mathematical. Solving KenKen or Sudoku puzzles individually can be a relaxing way to engage with math. So can playing games with friends and family. There's mathematical thinking in traditional card games such as rummy, hearts, or bridge; traditional board games like chess or go; and also in commercial games such as *Set*, *Blokus*, or *Yahtzee*. If teachers have fun while doing math, it is easier for them to help children have fun while doing math.

The Bottom Line

Math anxiety gets in the way of math learning and math doing for many people. If teachers can alleviate or prevent it in themselves, children, and families, then the next generation will be more successful in school and life.

   Research has not solved the "chicken or egg" problem—whether high math anxiety or poor math abilities comes first. However, the research is clear that once either is established, the two influence one another. Since we don't know which comes first, teachers need to work both to reduce children's experience of anxiety about math and to increase children's competence in doing math. The more approaches children have to make sense of mathematical situations, the more likely they will be to be able to solve problems and, hopefully, the less math anxious they will feel.

Key Research Studies Discussed

Berkowitz, T., Schaeffer, M. W., Maloney, E. A., Peterson, L., Gregor, C., Levine, S. C., and Beilock, S. L. (2015). Math at home adds up to achievement at school. *Science, 350*(6257),196–198. doi:10.1126/science. aac7427

Maloney, E. A., Ansari, D., and Fugelsang, J. A. (2011). The effect of mathematics anxiety on the processing of numerical magnitude. *Quarterly Journal of Experimental Psychology, 64*(1), 10–16.

Maloney, E. A., Ramirez, G., Gunderson, E. A., Levine, S. C., and Beilock, S. L. (2015). Intergenerational effects of parents' math anxiety on children's math achievement and anxiety. *Psychological Science, 26*(9),1480–8. doi:10.1177/0956797615592630

Ramirez, G., Chang, H., Maloney, E. A., Levine, S., and Beilock, S. L. (2016). On the relationship between math anxiety and math achievement in early elementary school: The role of problem solving strategies. *Journal of Experimental Child Psychology, 141*, 83-100.

Other References

Chang, H., and Beilock, S. L. (2016). The math anxiety-math performance link and its relation to individual and environmental factors: A review of current behavioral and psychophysiological research. *Current Opinion in Behavioral Sciences, 10*, 33–38.

Hembree, R. (1990). The nature, effects, and relief of mathematics anxiety. *Journal for Research in Mathematics Education, 21*(1), 33–46.

Maloney, E. A., Sattizahn, J. R., and Beilock, S. L. (2014). Anxiety and cognition. *Wiley Interdisciplinary Reviews: Cognitive Science, 5*(4), 403–411.

Maloney, E. A., Schaeffer, M. W., and Beilock, S. L. (2013). Mathematics anxiety and stereotype threat: Shared mechanisms, negative consequences, and promising interventions. *Research in Mathematics Education, 15*, 115–128.

Conclusion: What Have We Learned?

Jennifer S. McCray, Janet Eisenband Sorkin, and Jie-Qi Chen

Anyone who doubts the richness and complexity of early childhood mathematics need look no further than this volume. Together, our featured researchers and teachers create a portrait of early math teaching and learning that is nuanced, complex, and fascinating. In part because the earliest mathematics is focused on the development of very foundational kinds of abstractions—like the concept of "three-ness"—early math is simultaneously the province of four year olds and cognitive developmental scientists.

The kind of early thinking that makes mathematics possible provides templates for the abilities to abstract, compare, order, and generalize. The first times we use mathematics—a tool which it took humans, as a species, thousands of years to develop—we build mental schemas that will support our organization and analysis of everything else we will learn. Math achievement at kindergarten entry is the best predictor we know of for later school success, and that is likely because early mathematical understandings are so far-reaching in many different kinds of thought and learning. The earliest math learning is probably best described as profound, rather than either complex or simple: the concepts are very large, and somewhat "tricky." For these reasons, there is a lot to study about the knowledge and how it develops, and there will long be a need for work that connects new findings in cognitive research with early math teachers and teaching practice.

This book has been one such attempt to link developmental science to education. There are of course, other structures and mechanisms that share this purpose: teacher education classes, professional development seminars, and other adult learning settings can focus on helping teachers better understand children's learning processes.

Further, the findings of cognitive developmental research related to early math are often reflected in math curricula and learning materials, which provide an additional avenue for their expression. This book, however, is meant to yield something distinct, both by gathering a carefully selected set of research findings in one place, and by fostering a more direct, interactive experience between those who uncover new knowledge about how children learn, and those who spend their days directly helping them to do so.

To better examine these contributions, we here analyze the book in terms of two questions: 1) What generalizations with teaching implications, if any, can be usefully gleaned by looking across the various research topics? 2) What kinds of knowledge and learning accrued to both teachers and researchers via the process that generated the book?

Synthesizing the Research for Teaching Implications

Several common themes emerged from the research discussed in these chapters. We will address them in terms of three categories: types of input, children's strategies, and discrepancies in adults' understanding of children's learning.

Input Matters

Perhaps the most recurrent idea the research presented was that specific types of input make a difference in helping children gain math skills. Hearing mathematical language, playing with certain types of objects, seeing and using gestures while communicating about math, and even utilizing one's fingers to compute sums—these are all experiences that help children figure out math ideas. It is not simply that children are born with or without an aptitude toward math: the input they receive and the experiences they have clearly influence their math learning.

Several chapters also suggest that receiving input in *certain combinations*, such as language with gesture, language with objects, or related arithmetic problems in close succession, seems to help children make connections between ideas and build understanding. Mix and Uttal's research goes further to show that *making the links very explicit*, either via the physical structure of the input (muffin tins having "containers" that fit whiffle balls perfectly) or by literally explaining how things are related to one another (e.g., "Look—this is Big Snoopy's big couch, and this is Little Snoopy's little couch. They're just the same.") can help children connect the ideas. When the nature of the objects is such that children will focus on the objects separately (the frogs and the whiffle balls) or only on the object and not the related idea (manipulatives presented as toys), children are less likely to be making abstractions.

We also learn that to be helpful, input must be received over an *extended period of time*. Levine's research indicated that just hearing number words a handful of times is not enough to help children learn about the cardinalities of the number words. Likewise, Baroody found that children need to spend many months—often a couple of years—counting on their fingers before they figure out advanced strategies for addition. Perhaps this is one reason Uttal argues that in terms of mathematical manipulatives, limiting the input to fewer *types* is helpful. Children cannot possibly spend extended lengths of time using every kind of manipulative out there. Instead, Uttal argues, selecting one or two types and using these over and over again will help children make connections to the concepts.

Finally, the Baroody and Maloney chapters point out that input is not always positive, and is not always *cognitive* in nature. Baroody argues that certain types of input (e.g., drilling of facts/timed tests) do not tend to promote learning, in part because they are inefficient, and in part because they are unpleasant. Moreover, the research discussed in the Maloney chapter suggests that when adults have anxiety about math, the input they provide to children can have negative effects on learning. On the flip side, this chapter also points out a tool (the Bedtime Math app) that seems to help adults with math anxiety provide input to children that is more beneficial.

Children's Strategies

A second recurring theme in the chapters is the significance of children's use of different strategies in solving problems. The Baroody chapter emphasized that children can discover new addition and subtraction strategies on their own, especially if given certain input, and that the ability to apply a strategy to a new problem is a sign of true fluency. However, from the Siegler chapter we learn that even if children have figured out a new strategy, they still may use old strategies, and in fact can benefit from knowing multiple strategies.

The Maloney and Mix chapters tell us that certain factors may influence children's use of strategies. In the Maloney chapter we learned that anxiety can get in the way of children using certain strategies—they might be less likely to take risks with new, more efficient, strategies when they are anxious. And the Mix chapter suggests that combinations of diverse experiences can trigger children to use certain strategies: working on spatial problems may trigger children to use spatially related strategies in an algebra task, which in turn help them solve the problem.

Discrepancies in Adults' Understanding of Children's Thinking

A third theme is the ways that there are sometimes inconsistencies between what we think a child knows and what she or he actually knows. In two chapters we saw that children may know things that we don't necessarily see in our assessments, but that we can sometimes detect them in unconventional ways. For example, Levine found that a non-verbal task revealed knowledge about number and operations in some children that was not detected using a verbal task. Similarly, Goldin-Meadow found that children can have implicit knowledge about numbers and about conservation, and that this knowledge can reveal itself through mismatches between their gestures and their words.

On the other hand, in some chapters we see that children might not have the level of understanding that we assume they have. For example, the Uttal chapter shows that even connections that may seem very obvious to adults (such as a Little Snoopy in a scale model representing a Big Snoopy in an actual room) may not be obvious at all to young children. Siegler's research tells us that one or two behaviors do not always give us the full picture of children's understanding: we can't assume that because we have seen a child use a new, more efficient strategy, that he or she has moved on to a new "stage" and will always use that strategy. To really understand where the child is, we need to monitor closely and for a long period of time.

Analyzing the Process: New Learning for Teachers and Researchers

As is described more thoroughly in the introduction, we used a unique process to generate our "conversations" between researchers and teachers. Briefly, after selecting early math-related cognitive developmental topics and the researchers we felt could represent them, we interviewed the researchers and summarized relevant studies, working closely with them to ensure accuracy. We then held a bi-weekly seminar with a small group of teacher participants, who read and reviewed these summaries, and met with us to discuss the material and provide feedback—mostly questions the research raised for them and ideas they had about how it connected to their own work. We shared their questions with researchers, who either provided written responses or spoke to us about their ideas, and these questions and their answers constituted the middle section of each content-focused chapter. We followed this with our summation of the ideas teachers had for applications of the research in their teaching practice. Throughout, we sprinkled comments from both teachers and researchers, to give more direct voice to their different perspectives than is commonly available. Below, we outline the kinds of learning we believe resulted.

Teacher Learning

We observed many instances in which teachers encountered new ideas that they felt would impact their work. For example, learning from Goldin-Meadow's work that children can exhibit "mismatches" between gesture and speech, and that this may indicate readiness to learn, was a non-obvious game-changer with clear implications for teachers. We saw that Siegler's work increased the teachers' awareness of the simultaneous use of multiple strategies in their young charges, and that this inspired renewed plans to encourage use of and discussion about different types of strategies in their classrooms. In each of the seminar discussions, teachers recognized the power that their choices and actions have to support the early learning of mathematics: the work validates early childhood teachers' roles in a climate that sometimes dismisses their impact.

Teachers also learned about research processes. Early childhood teachers are generally not required to have graduate degrees. Many do, but even then, their exposure to research vocabulary, its dilemmas and processes, may be limited. Teachers in our seminar spent several months engaging in the thinking processes of researchers. Chapters are written to follow a continuous line of thought, as in, "Once we learned X, we knew we needed to understand Y," and include comments and reflections from the researchers themselves, personalizing this "hunt" for understanding. We also take the time to clarify difficult and important concepts, such as "cardinality," introduce particular analytic approaches, such as "microgenetic," and engage teachers in the kinds of puzzles about causality ("We know they occur together, but which causes which?") that are the common province of developmental scientists. The teachers were interested in the research process and raised important questions about the methods throughout the seminar.

Researcher Learning

We also found, however, that there were moments when the researchers gained insight from the questions and comments provided by teachers. For example, when the seminar teachers suggested that part of what determines whether a manipulative plays a useful versus distracting role might be the complexity of the task at hand, David Uttal responded that there was little systematic study of this question, suggesting it might be a good direction for new research. His responses also noted teachers' "intriguing" idea that manipulatives might be especially supportive in constructing early notions of cardinality. Similarly, teachers asked Kelly Mix to parse her idea of "slotted-ness" to make clear the role of pairing between objects and slots. Was it not also important, teachers wondered, that the multiple slots are part of a singular object, suggesting the grouping of single items into a unified amount? Mix was reminded of a previous plan—never implemented—to study this question.

Researchers also learned more about teaching from this project. The theme of how best to help dual language learners was raised quite frequently, reminding our scientists to consider this complexity. Teachers' comments and questions evoked classroom dilemmas and adult decision-making in a way that was often provocative for researchers. For example, when teachers asked Susan Goldin-Meadow about the difference between teaching techniques such as TPR (Total Physical Response), which involves the conscious use of gesture, and unplanned, unconscious gesture, it led her to ponder whether teachers' unconscious gestures could be studied to provide new ideas for TPR. Our experience overall was that feedback from the teachers often inspired and motivated the researchers, and sometimes encouraged them to boil down their findings into one or two practical recommendations.

In Sum

Bringing these two sets of people together is not easy or convenient. They work in different contexts that rarely cross over, they have different (though related) professional goals, and there are limited structures that support their collaboration. As early math education researchers, we are in the privileged position of commonly interacting with them both, and this book was an attempt to help them communicate their ideas with one another.

We found, in general, that both parties were genuinely interested in and enthusiastic about the process. Teachers came to sessions after a full day of work, ready to engage in active discussion about studies that were not always easy to understand. Many commented at the end of the last session that they would miss these stimulating conversations with peers. Researchers appreciated teachers' insights, and were eager to answer their questions and offer suggestions. In our experience, it is a real honor to work with both these groups of dedicated professionals, whose passion and commitment are what keep the field of early math moving forward. The ideas for classroom practice that teachers generated in each chapter are testimony to what can arise when there is more of a connection between the two groups. We sincerely hope this book may inspire other efforts to foster the kind of powerful collaborations between psychologists and teachers that can really improve early math learning.

Index

Note: Page numbers in *italic* indicate a figure, and page numbers in **bold** indicate a table on the corresponding page.

Taylor & Francis Group
an **informa** business

Taylor & Francis eBooks

www.taylorfrancis.com

A single destination for eBooks from Taylor & Francis
with increased functionality and an improved user
experience to meet the needs of our customers.

90,000+ eBooks of award-winning academic content in
Humanities, Social Science, Science, Technology, Engineering,
and Medical written by a global network of editors and authors.

TAYLOR & FRANCIS EBOOKS OFFERS:

A streamlined
experience for
our library
customers

A single point
of discovery
for all of our
eBook content

Improved
search and
discovery of
content at both
book and
chapter level

REQUEST A FREE TRIAL
support@taylorfrancis.com

 Routledge
Taylor & Francis Group

 CRC Press
Taylor & Francis Group